Happy Easter!

Love God an
Love Other

Mr. Jim
Paw-Paw

Just Like Jesus

Christian Discipleship
For
Children and Youth

"We are never too old or never too young to become a disciple of Jesus"

Just Like Jesus

Walter B. Pennington
penningtonwalter@bellsouth.net

Unless otherwise indicated, all scriptures are taken from The Children's Living Bible and are printed in bold *italics*.

Acknowledgments

I am grateful to God for presenting me with the opportunity and privilege to deliver His message to our children and youth for this end-time season of correction and restoration. Our children and youth must gain their 'spiritual footing' by realizing their need and ordained purpose in God's kingdom. I am very grateful for the oversight of the Holy Spirit, without which this writing would not have been possible.

I am grateful for my granddaughters, Jaylah, Jordyn, and Wyntor Pennington. They provided spiritual insight from a youthful perspective that was needed for this writing. They are indeed gifts from God to humanity.

Also, I thank my lovely wife, Jackie, my sister Dorothy and my daughter Kevalyn for their support, for taking the time to proofread the manuscript, and for offering their invaluable insight.

May God continue to give guidance along their pathways through life.

---

[3]

Just Like Jesus

<u>Contents</u>

---

*"And the child grew and became strong; he was
filled with wisdom, and the grace of God was
upon him."*
Luke 2:40 (NIV)

Yes, you too can accomplish
the unbelievable!
(John 14:12)
Now, the journey begins.

Introduction

Not much was written in the Bible about the childhood of Jesus. What was written is found in the book of Luke.

If we want to become a disciple of Jesus and grow to be like Him, we need to start learning about Him as early as possible, even in our childhood. We are never too old or never too young to be like Jesus.

When we become like Jesus, we are then called a "Christian." Most people define a Christian as a follower of Jesus. Though this is true, it is not the complete Biblical understanding and is misleading. Because of this misunderstanding, most people in America consider themselves "Christians." To be true to the understanding of the Bible, a "**Christian**" is a person who has the character (everything about a person that makes them who they are) of Jesus, or a person who is "Christlike," or "just like Jesus."

When a person commits their life to Jesus, they become a believer. A **"believer"** believes what the Bible says about Jesus and trusts those things. A believer receives Jesus as their Lord and Savior and follows Him in faith, love, holiness, and obedience *(these will be discussed)*. However, they are not yet "Christlike" or Christian. They are not yet 'just like Jesus.' They must grow and develop into His likeness as they commit their lives to Him and learn about Him. However, all true believers will go to Heaven to live with Jesus forever when they leave this world.

As stated, a believer has faith in God. **"Faith"** in God is complete trust and confidence in God. We show our faith in God when we trust Him to do what He says in the Bible that He will do. We show our faith in God by believing everything that He says. Our faith in God is revealed in the confidence and hope that we have as we live each day, no matter the surrounding conditions.

You may ask, "What is a disciple?" A **"disciple"** is a person who wants to be just like someone else that they look up to and admire. So they follow them, dedicate their lives to learning as much as they can about them, and do everything possible to be just like them or a reflection of them. So a disciple of Jesus is someone who wants to be just like Jesus, even when He was a child.

You may say, "But Jesus was the Son of God, and I am not the Son of God, so I cannot be just like Jesus." Yes, you can because we are all children of God. He is our heavenly Father. He made each of us, knows all about us, and wants us to be like Jesus.

Yes, Jesus was the Son of God. This means that He did not have a human father like the rest of us. He was born and raised on earth just as you and I. We all have a human father and mother. We also have a heavenly Father Who made us and everything else in this world. Some of us may or may not know much about our human father, but the Bible teaches us a lot about our heavenly Father, and it teaches us a lot about Jesus.

Jesus was as human as you and I. He was tempted to do wrong things just like all of us. He felt pain and hurt, just like all of us. He grew from being a baby to become an adult, just like all of us. He learned from others, just like all of us. He had brothers and sisters just like many of us do. He had a purpose in life given to Him by His Father in Heaven, just like all of us. Our heavenly Father has given each of us a purpose and a reason to live for Him while we are here on the earth. After we finish living on earth, all of us, as believers and obedient children, will be with Him in Heaven forever, where we will receive new bodies and no longer feel pain, hurt, and suffering.

"**Heaven**" is a beautiful place that our heavenly Father made for all of us to live with Him after we finish His business of living for Jesus on earth. Like Jesus, He has assigned each of us a purpose and placed us here on the earth. We may not all look alike, act alike, or think alike. We may come from different races, places, and backgrounds. Our differences are the beauty of this world. To our heavenly Father, we look like a mixture of beautiful flowers planted in His garden (earth). We are all His children. We are brothers and sisters, and He loves each of us the same. All of us are important and have a special purpose for our lives given by our Father in Heaven.

What is our business on earth? **Our business is to become like Jesus,** so people who don't know anything about Jesus and our heavenly Father will want to know them because they know us and see the character of Jesus and our heavenly Father in us. Jesus loves as our heavenly Father loves. We must learn to love everyone as Jesus loves everyone. But first, we must learn to love ourselves because our heavenly Father loves each of us, and we are special to Him.

You may say, "Yes, I want to be a disciple of Jesus. So what does the Bible teach us about Jesus when He was a child?"

In the second chapter of Luke, we find a story about Jesus when He was twelve years old. This is the only story that we have in the Bible of His childhood. So what can we learn from this story that will help us to become His disciple and be like Jesus? Let's find out.

As a child, Jesus lived in a small village called Nazareth with his brothers and sisters, His earthly father Joseph and His mother, Mary. Each year they would travel sixty-five miles to Jerusalem for a festival (celebration) called the Passover. Passover was one of three yearly festivals held in Jerusalem that honored God. Every male was required to attend these festivals. Passover was the most important of the three festivals. Jesus and His family would travel to Jerusalem with other relatives and friends in a caravan. A **caravan** is a group of people traveling together.

We find this story of the child Jesus in the book of Luke, Chapter 2, verses 41-52. Our Bible says,

"Every year Jesus' parents traveled to Jerusalem for the Feast of Passover. When he was twelve years old, they went up as they always did for the Feast. When it was over and they left for home, the child Jesus stayed behind in Jerusalem, but his parents didn't know it. Thinking he was somewhere in the company of pilgrims, they journeyed for a whole day and then began looking for him among relatives and

neighbors. When they didn't find him, they went back to Jerusalem, looking for him.

The next day they found him in the Temple seated among the teachers, listening to them and asking questions. The teachers were all quite taken with him, impressed with the sharpness of his answers. But his parents were not impressed; they were upset and hurt.

His mother said, "Young man, why have you done this to us? Your father and I have been half out of our minds looking for you."

He said, "Why were you looking for me? Didn't you know that I had to be here, dealing with the things of my Father?" But they had no idea what he was talking about.

So he went back to Nazareth with them, and lived obediently with them. His mother held these things dearly, deep within herself. And Jesus matured, growing up in both body and spirit [(tall and wise) (NIV)]*, blessed by both God and people"* (Message Bible).

As already stated, this is the only story written in the Bible about Jesus when He was a child. So what can we learn from this story that will help us become His disciple and be like Jesus? Again, let's find out.

(Prayers and questions for discussion are provided at the end of each chapter. We truly believe that prayer is the most important privilege that God has given to the disciples of Jesus. As disciples of Jesus, we must begin to pray about everything and at all times. Prayer can change things.)

Prayer:

Heavenly Father, I start this reading because I want to know You better and realize my purpose in Your kingdom on earth. I want to know Jesus as not just my Savior, Lord, and friend, but as my model for how I live my life for You. Open my understanding that I may receive knowledge and wisdom beyond my age. I ask this not for my sake only, but for You and Your kingdom on earth as others will see Jesus living in me and be drawn to You. Amen.

Questions:

1. How do most people define "Christian?"
2. What is the Bible's understanding of "Christian?"
3. What does it mean to be a believer in Christ?
4. What is a disciple of Christ? Explain.
5. What is faith in God? Explain.
6. Where do believers go when they leave this world?
7. Though we may all be different, how do we look to our heavenly Father?
8. What is meant by, "We are all brothers and sisters?"
9. What is our business on earth? Why is this important?

Chapter 1

Taking Care of Our Responsibilities

"When Jesus was twelve years old he accompanied his parents to Jerusalem for the annual Passover Festival, which they attended each year." - Luke 2:42

As a child, Jesus took care of His responsibilities. As we have already written, there were three festivals each year in Jerusalem that celebrated God. God required all males to attend these festivals. Though Jesus was only a male child, He attended these festivals with His parents each year because young boys were also required to attend. Therefore, Jesus honored His responsibility and willingly attended with His parents. These festivals honored the Father, and Jesus always wanted to do what honored and pleased His heavenly Father. Jesus learned to please His heavenly Father from His childhood, and it was His joy to please Him until He left the earth and returned to Heaven.

Everyone has responsibilities given to them by other people, including their parents and guardians, and everyone has responsibilities given to them by God the Father that they must honor.

[13]

Our parents have many responsibilities. They are responsible for taking care of us, keeping us safe, and providing for our needs. When we need something, most of us know that we can ask our parents. They may not give us everything that we want, but, as their children, they are responsible for providing us with what we need. When we say that they are **responsible**, it means that it is their duty. It means that they are expected to take care of us and do what is required for our well-being. They are required to do these things and many more things that we may not realize. The government requires that they do certain things, and God requires that they do certain things. They will be held accountable by humanity and God for what they do or fail to do. We should always let our parents know how much we appreciate the many things they do for us out of love and responsibility.

God made this world, placed humans (us) in charge, and gave us the power, right, and responsibility to maintain it. This meant that God gave us His authority. **Authority** is the right to give orders, make decisions, or take action when needed. Though we have God's authority, most of the problems in this world happen because many people do not honor their responsibilities. Many do not honor their responsibilities to each other or to God. If everyone honored their responsibilities, the world would be a better place to live, and God would be pleased.

God gives us His responsibilities in the Bible. They are called commandments. **Commandments** are God's rules that we must honor and follow (obey). Because they come from God, they are called **Divine** rules.

[14]

As disciples of Jesus, we must obey God's commandments. **Obey** means to carry out the commands, orders, instructions, or wishes of someone else. It simply means to do what you are told to do. As we must obey our parents, we also must obey God.

****

Just as our parents have responsibilities, as children and youth, we also have responsibilities. Our parents give us things to do that we are responsible for doing. Also, God gives us commandments that we are responsible for doing. God is pleased when we honor our responsibilities. Many of us do not like responsibilities, but responsibilities help us develop our **character** (the things that make us who we are and make us different from each other, our makeup). Our responsibilities and how we manage them will determine who we will become and the quality and success of our lives for the remainder of our time on earth.

As school-age children and youth, we are responsible for doing our homework and our classroom work. At home, we may be responsible for cleaning our room or washing dishes after family meals. We may be responsible for folding our clothes. We are responsible for bathing and keeping our bodies clean. We are responsible for brushing our teeth and combing our hair. If we are older, we may be responsible for cutting the grass or ironing our clothes. If we have pets, we may be responsible for feeding them and taking care of their needs. Our parents will give us responsibilities, things that we are required to do.

Our Bible also gives us responsibilities or commandments. It tells us that we must obey our

[15]

parents. We must honor our father and mother (Ephesians 6:1-2). With all of the responsibilities that we have, it is important to know which are more important so we can **prioritize** them (responsibilities that are more important than others).

Our Bible gives us the most important responsibility for all of God's children. In the books of Matthew, Mark, and Luke, Jesus gave us our most important responsibility or commandment from God. In Mark 12, verses 29-30, Jesus said, *"The Lord our God is the one and only God. And you must love him with all your heart and soul and mind and strength."*

Since this is our most important responsibility, we need to understand what it means to love God with all our heart, soul, mind, and strength.

We love God with all our **heart** when we love Him more than anything else in this world, including ourselves. It means that we are ready to give up, do or suffer anything to please Him. When we love God with all our heart, pleasing and honoring Him are our primary goals and reasons for life. Our love for Him is shown through our obedience to His holy word and love for all others (1st John 4:20-21).

We love God with all our **soul** when all of our living is just for Him. All of our soul simply means all of our life. We must see our life in this world as belonging to God and completely dedicated to His service and glory. We trust Him for maintaining our life because He said in the Bible that He would do so when we honor and receive Him as our shepherd (Psalms 23:3).

[16]

We love God with all our **mind** when we desire only to know God and His will for our life. Our mind is totally fixed on understanding and knowing Him. Everything that we study, we see it in relation to Him. All of our thoughts are in relation to Him. When we love God with all our mind, we think of Him at all times as a way of life, no matter what we are doing.

We love God with all our **strength** when all of the powers of our bodies are used for His purpose. Though we may be doing many things, all of our labor is dedicated to Him and meant for His glory. It means that we only act in ways or only do physical things that bring attention to how great God really is. We dedicate and sacrifice our bodies only to honor and glorify God.

In addition to loving God with all our heart, soul, mind, and strength, Jesus gave his disciples a new responsibility or commandment that God had not required before. God always required that we love each other. God had commanded us to *"Love others as well as you love yourself"* (Mark 12:31) (Message Bible). However, Jesus wanted us to love each other even more. In John 13, verse 34, Jesus said to His disciples, *"Love each other just as much as I love you."* Jesus loves all others more than He loves Himself. In verse thirty-five, Jesus said, *"Your strong love for each other will prove to the world that you are my disciples."* Jesus made these two responsibilities or commandments His foundational [(base upon which everything else is built and done) (ref. 1st Corinthians 13:1-3)] requirements for becoming His disciple. To become His disciple, we must honor and obey the responsibilities or commandments that He gave.

[17]

Jesus wanted us to know that showing love as He did is our greatest responsibility as His disciples. We must love God and all others just as Jesus did and still does. As disciples of Jesus, everything that we do for God must be done in total love for God and total love for all others. If we do anything for God but don't love everyone, we dishonor God. To **dishonor God** means to disrespect and bring shame upon God. When we love God and all others more than we love ourselves, our love will show the world that we are disciples of Jesus.

****

God made us, and He owns us. Without Him, we cannot provide or care for ourselves. Because of this, He accepts responsibility for us when we commit our lives to Him. God loves us, provides for us, and protects us. God is a wonderful and caring Father. There is no other God in the world but our heavenly Father. He is the true God of this world (ref. Mark 12:29). All other gods are **false gods** (not real) that are made and created in our minds and by our hands. Anything that humans can create in their minds or make with their hands is not a real God. We should not honor it, worship it, or have anything to do with it. God has commanded in the Bible that we should have no other gods. This is the first commandment that God gave to us. God commanded us in Exodus 20:3, *"You shall have no other gods before me"* (NIV).

****

Note: When we are talking about our heavenly Father as God, we use the capital letter "G." When we are talking about all other gods, we use the lower case "g."

****

[18]

What are some other gods that we can have? Other gods (false gods) can come in many different forms. Anything in this world can become a god when we begin to worship it. There is a term that is often used in the Bible that is applied to false gods. The word is "idol." An **idol** is anything loved more than God, wanted more than God, enjoyed more than God, or treasured more than God. It can be a person or thing that we love and admire more than God. The worship of any other thing or person other than God is called **"idolatry."** As servants of God, **worship** is showing ultimate devotion, honor, and respect for God only. As we have already said, God commanded in the Bible that we shall have no other gods before Him.

The Bible gives many warnings about idolatry. Our Bible tells us in 1st Corinthians 10:14, *"So dear friends, carefully avoid idol worship of every kind."* Also, it tells us in 1st John 5:21, *"Dear children, keep away from anything that might take God's place in your hearts."* Our Bible informs us that it is a sin to worship anything else in this world. In obedience to the will of God, we must only worship Him.

What is sin? **Sin** is disobeying God's instructions in the Bible.

If we own anything in this world that we love more than God, that thing has become an idol to us, and we should get rid of it and ask God to forgive us of that sin. We should ask God to help us not love anything in this world more than we love Him. We should also ask God to show us anything in our possession or this world that we have allowed to become an idol. Once God reveals it to us, we must get rid of it or remove ourselves from it.

[19]

What are some things in our lives that can become an idol?

1. Items of clothing or footwear such as tennis shoes that we love more than God.
2. Toys or games that we spend more time with than we spend with God.
3. A person that we admire more than we admire God, such as a rock star, a movie star, an athlete, or even a close friend or family member.
4. Money, jewelry, and precious stones can become idols when we begin to love them and value them more than we do God.
5. Cell phones, iPads, iPhones, and social media can become idols when we love to spend more time using them than we spend with God.
6. Televisions and sports can become idols when we love watching them and spending more time watching them than we spend with God.
7. Our homes, jobs, and hobbies can become idols when we love them more than we love God.
8. Our cars and vehicles can become idols when we love and care for them more than we do for God.
9. Even church buildings and religious activities can become idols when we love them more than we love God.
10. We must love, honor, and obey our parents and guardians. However, they can become our idols when we begin to love them more than we love God.
11. We can become our idols when we love ourselves more than we love God.

These are just a few examples of idols. Again, idols can come in many different forms, so we must be very careful not to have any idols in our lives.

****

There is a story in the Bible about obedience, faith, and the Biblically correct response to idolatry (Dan. 3).

There was a king whose name was Nebuchadnezzar. He made a golden statue that was ninety feet high and nine feet wide. King Nebuchadnezzar loved this statue, and to him, it was his god. This statue was his idol. He called everyone in his kingdom to come together to show everyone this great statue he had made. He had it announced that every time the band would start to play music, everyone had to fall flat on the ground to worship his statue.

When the band started to play, everyone but three men fell to the ground and worshiped the statue as the king commanded. King Nebuchadnezzar was told that these three men did not do as he commanded. The names of these three men were Shadrach, Meshach, and Abednego. These three men loved God more than anything else. **Our love for God is shown in our obedience to Him.** Because they loved God and were obedient to Him, they would not worship anything else or anybody but God. Because they had learned about God, they knew the commandments that God had given. They knew that God had commanded in Exodus 34:17, *"You must have nothing to do with idols."* Also, God had commanded in Leviticus 26:1, *"You must have no idols; carved images, obelisks, or shaped stones, for I am the Lord your God."* So, in obedience to the commands of God, they refused to fall

[21]

down and worship the statue that King Nebuchadnezzar had made.

King Nebuchadnezzar became very angry with these three men. **People will often become angry with you when you refuse to honor, worship, or recognize their idols**. The king gave them one more chance to worship his golden statue. He told them that he would have them thrown into a flaming furnace if they refused to worship his statue again.

In response to the king's threat, Shadrach, Meshach, and Abednego said to king Nebuchadnezzar, *"O Nebuchadnezzar, we are not worried about what will happen to us. If we are thrown into the flaming furnace, our God is able to deliver us; and he will deliver us out of your hand. We will never under any circumstance serve your gods or worship the golden statue you have erected."*

In the Bible, God promised His faithful servants that He would fight their battles (Deuteronomy 20:4), and He would be their shield in times of trouble (Psalms 3:3). These men were obedient and had faith in God.

****

In the introduction of this book, we defined faith as complete trust and confidence in God. We show our faith in God when we trust Him to do what he says in the Bible that He will do. We show our faith in God by believing everything that He says. We must study the Bible to know what to expect and what not to expect from God. Sometimes, we ask God to do things for us that He has not promised in the Bible that He will do. These three men knew that God had promised His protection to His faithful servants. They had faith that

[22]

God would honor His promises. So we must pray to God according to what the Bible says about Him.

****

After the three men acknowledged their faith in God, the king became even more furious. **When we truly show our faith in God, many times, nonbelievers will become hostile to us.** The king became so furious that he had the furnace heated up seven times hotter than usual. He had the three men bound with ropes and threw them into the flaming furnace. The flames were so hot that they killed the king's soldiers as they threw them into the furnace. Amazingly, Shadrach, Meshach, and Abednego were not killed in the flames as the king had hoped. They did not even get burned in the fire because an angel of God protected them. The angel of God entered into the furnace with them and shielded them from the flames (Psalms 28:7). God proved to be faithful to His word.

Not only were these three men not killed, but while in the furnace, they were not even burned. When they came out of the furnace, they did not even smell like smoke. When king Nebuchadnezzar saw them, he said, *"Blessed be the God of Shadrach, Meshach, and Abednego, for he sent his angel to deliver his trusting servants when they defied the king's commandment, and were willing to die rather than serve or worship any god except their own"* (Again, this story is found in the third chapter of the book of Daniel. Take the time to read it and study it as a model for obedience, faith in God, and guidance for responding to idolatry).

God protected these three men because they loved Him more than anything else and refused to worship

[23]

anything besides Him. As servants of God, we must be like Shadrach, Meshach, and Abednego and refuse to allow any idols into our lives, and God will bless us.

****

We serve a wonderful and caring God. There is no other god like Him who loves us and can do the things that He does. Our heavenly Father made us and made the world and everything in it for our needs and His pleasure. We were created by and for Him. No other god can do what our God has done and continues to do every day.

As His servants, He heals our bodies when we are sick, and He restores us when we need restoring. He provides the water that we need to drink by sending rain from the clouds to the earth. He provides the food that we eat by putting the nutrients (substance required for growth) in the soil that makes things grow. He provides the cattle, poultry, and all of the meats that we eat each day. He made the sun that shines to give light to our days and provides heat to the earth to keep us warm. He allows us to sleep at night, and He enables us to wake every morning. He restores our minds so we can learn more about Him and learn and remember what our teachers teach us in the church and school classrooms. He allows us to feel through our hands and hearts, hear through our ears, smell through our noses, and see through our eyes. Without Him, we cannot and play and do everything we do every day. These are just some of the things that God does for us. It is impossible to list everything that God does. No one else in this world can do what our God does and who loves and cares for us as our God does. Therefore, we should love Him more than anything or anybody else, respect Him, honor Him, and obey Him.

As a brief review of our love for God (our most important responsibility), when God said that we must love Him with all of our heart, soul, mind, and strength, He meant that we must show our love for Him through everything about us. Our love for God must be shown in everything that we do, in everything that we say, and in all of our thoughts and interests. We are to love no one else or nothing else more than we love God. As much as we love our parents and ourselves, we are to love God even more. It means that there is nothing that we won't give up for Him, nothing that we won't do for Him, and nothing that we won't suffer for Him. We should find all of our joy and purpose in life in serving and pleasing Him.

One important requirement for Christian discipleship is that we must see all of our possessions (the things that we have), including our bodies, as not belonging to us, but belonging to God, to do with them only what He desires and allows us to do (1st Cor. 6:19). So, we must take care of our bodies and not do anything to them that God would disapprove. The Bible tells us that we own nothing in this world, and God owns everything, including all of the money we receive (Psalm 24:1, 50:12, 89:11). We may work to obtain the things and money we have, but they belong to God. We are stewards of all of the things that we have, including money. A **steward** is a person who takes care of or manages another person's money, things, or business. After we leave this world, we must explain to God how

[25]

we handled all of the things we now have. He will then reward us for managing His things as the Bible requires of us or punish us if we were selfish and did not manage them as the Bible requires of us.

We must learn to see God in everything, which helps us think of Him at all times. We must keep our minds on Him as a way of life, no matter what is going on around us. Truly, this is a new way of living.

Indeed, it is a great challenge to become a disciple of Jesus because it requires seeing everything, even life itself, much different from the world. So, when we spend valuable (precious) time playing ungodly video games, watching worldly television, or entertaining the worldliness of social media, through them, we will only see things as the world does. Disciples of Jesus are not **worldly** (Living to please ourselves through the things and pleasures of this world and living outside of God's laws or what the Bible allows) (James 4:4). As the boy Jesus, we should only seek activities that please God, that will help us develop into the image of Christ. **We must avoid all things of this world that draw our attention away from God at all costs.** To become a disciple of Jesus requires much sacrifice. We must dedicate ourselves to Jesus so that He can live through us as the hope for this world. We should never forget that we can never sacrifice as much as Jesus has sacrificed for us. Jesus gave us all that He had. He gave His life for us by dying on the cross for the sins that we commit. Through His death, our sins are forgiven.

As a review, how much are we to love each other? Jesus said that we must love each other just as much as

He loves us. Jesus loves us so much that he cares for our needs above His own. To become His disciple, we must be willing to sacrifice our desires for the needs of all others. We must be willing to do everything in our power, through all possible legal and unsinful means, for the needs of all others. Whatever we would want others to do for us, we must be willing to do even more for them. In summary, to love all others as much as Jesus loves us means that we cannot be **selfish** (caring too much about ourselves and little about others). We must be willing to deny ourselves for the needs and the good of all others.

What does this level of love look like in our day-to-day lives as children and youth? Let's look at some imagined examples in today's world. We show the love of Jesus by:

1. Giving someone your last dollar because they need it.
2. Not just helping your mom wash dishes after a meal, but volunteering to wash them so that she would not have to wash them.
3. Not going to a party or event that you were invited to, and looking forward to attending, to stay home with a sick relative or friend.
4. Not wanting expensive tennis shoes, expensive clothes, or expensive hairstyles so that your parents could use the money saved to pay bills or buy other much-needed things.
5. Letting others go ahead of you or giving someone your place in a long line.
6. Saving your money to help feed a poor family.

7. Not just praying for yourself and your needs, but praying for the needs of all others before your own.
8. Making the time to help someone in need who may not have even asked for your help.
9. Giving someone else your most favorite possession because they needed it but did not have one.
10. Showing love and treating someone nice (blessing them) who may curse you or hate you.
11. Not hitting someone back who may physically hit you; instead, forgiving them and praying for them (ref. Matthew 5:39, 44).
12. Giving someone who may have stolen something from you whatever else they need.

We could list many other imagined examples of this level of love. We encourage you to develop your list and make it a new way of life. This new life will become the beginning of you becoming just like Jesus. **Remember, to become a disciple of Jesus, we must love God with all our heart, soul, mind, and strength and love all others more than we love ourselves. As disciples of Christ, these are our most important responsibilities in life.**

The Bible tells us that Jesus only did the things that His heavenly Father wanted Him to do (ref. John 6:38). This dedication showed how much Jesus honored the responsibilities (commandments) that His Father gave Him. We, too, must commit to only doing the things that our heavenly Father wants us to do. We can pray to our heavenly Father and ask for His help to do **His will** (God's will is what He desires for us to do). We learn the things that He wants us to do by studying the Bible. The Bible gives us His will for our lives. When we love somebody who is responsible for us, as is God and our parents or guardians, we honor the responsibilities they give us and do our best to complete them and please them. Pleasing and serving others was the desire and the joy of Jesus, for He came to serve all others, not for others to serve Him (ref. Matthew 20:28, Mark 10:45).

As disciples of Christ, we must honor our responsibilities. Yes, we can be just like Jesus.

Prayer:

Heavenly Father, Thank You for your love. Thank You for giving me the necessary responsibilities to develop the character of Jesus within me. Thank you for revealing to me my most important responsibilities. I want to be a disciple of Jesus, so help me love You with all my heart, soul, mind, and strength. Also, help me to love all others as Jesus loves me. Firmly establish this foundation in my life from this day forward.

I ask that You reveal to me any idols in my life. Please, Father, help me remove myself from them to truly establish You as the only true God of my life.

Yes, I want to be Your servant by serving the needs of this world. Forgive me for being selfish and thinking of my needs before the needs of all others. With Your help, I will reveal You to the world through my new life in Christ from this day forward. Amen.

****

Questions:

1. What is the meaning of "responsible?"
2. List your responsibilities on a separate sheet of paper and describe your feelings about them.
3. What does it mean to have authority?
4. What are "commandments" in the Bible?
5. What is the meaning of "obey?"
6. What are the two primary responsibilities (commandments) that Jesus gave us to become His disciple?
7. What does it mean to love God with all your heart, soul, mind, and strength?
8. What does it mean to love all others as Jesus loves you?
9. What does it mean to dishonor God?
10. What is sin?
11. What is an idol? Define idolatry. List some things that can become idols in our lives.
12. Can you think of anything in your life that has become an idol? If yes, what should you do?
13. What is "worship?"
14. Name some ways that we can show faith in God.
15. What does the Bible mean by "God will fight your battles?" What is meant by "God will be your shield?" To whom is this promised?
16. Do we own ourselves, or does God own us?
17. What is a steward? Explain.
18. Can you think of anything that we may do to our bodies that God does not approve?
19. Can you explain the term "worldly?"
20. How do we learn the things that our heavenly Father wants us to do?

Chapter 2

Learning from Our Mistakes

"When it was over and they left for home, the child Jesus stayed behind in Jerusalem, but his parents didn't know it" (The Message Bible).
- Luke 2:43

As a child, Jesus made mistakes, but He learned from them. **Mistakes** are simply errors or poor decisions. It is important for all children and youth to know that Jesus made mistakes as a child. Though He was the Son of God, He was still as human as we are. As humans, we will make mistakes in life. But we must learn from them and not repeat them.

Growing up to become an adult is not easy. We will face many choices and decisions as we grow and mature. Some of our choices and decisions will be easy, and some will be very difficult. Growing up to become like Jesus is even more challenging because the ways of this world are not the ways of Jesus. Everyone in this world does not love each other as Jesus does and as we must learn. Everyone in this world does not love God as Jesus does, and as we also must learn. As disciples of Jesus, we must prepare ourselves to face the **hostilities** (a feeling of hate or dislike; no love) that this world has towards Jesus and those who love and

[31]

obey Him. We must grow and live in this world, but we must not give in to the pressures of becoming like this world. We must learn not to yield to the temptations of this world. **Temptation** is trying to get a person to do or want something that is wrong or is not allowed. To **yield to the temptations of this world** means giving way to or participating in the evil things in this world, things that God does not allow. We must always do our best to shield ourselves from the sinful temptations that we face every day. To be like Jesus, we must not give in to ungodly temptations, and in not doing so, learn to love everyone else, even those who may tempt us to do wrong or mistreat us.

As disciples of Jesus, we have an enemy, Satan, who hates God and everyone who loves God. Many people do not believe that Satan is real. Many believe that he is just a symbol (not real, but stands for) for evil. No, he is not a symbol. However, he is evil. Though we may not see him, he is a real being, and the Bible warns us about him and his evil ways. Almost half of the warnings are given in the New Testament in the Biblical books of Acts through Revelation. As a side reference, the two parts of the Bible are the Old Testament and the New Testament. The Bible **Testaments** are covenants or agreements between God and humanity that were given by God.

****

In the beginning, Satan was in Heaven with God before God created the world in which we live. He first appears in the Bible at the very beginning in the book of Genesis. Satan is believed to have been an archangel of God who served God in Heaven. An **archangel** is an angel of high rank. They have more power than other angels or humans.

[32]

Angels are beings that God created to serve Him and help us, His servants, when needed. All angels have more power than humans. As servants of God, He will often assign His angels to help us in life. They will often protect us when we are in trouble (ref. Daniel 3:28) or provide for other needs that we may have as we serve our heavenly Father here on earth. Because we don't often see them does not mean that they are not with us. However, angels do have the ability to appear before us when required (ref. Luke 1:11, 28-29).

It is believed that there are seven archangels in Heaven. The most popular archangels in the Bible are Michael and Gabriel. Angels can go back and forth between Heaven and earth. There are many angels in Heaven and on earth that serve God and humanity. Sometimes, they will deliver messages from God to someone on earth as they did with Daniel and Mary, the mother of Jesus. God often assigns them to protect and shelter His servants on earth from harm and danger. In addition to these assignments, they have many other responsibilities that God will give them.

While in Heaven, Satan was not happy in serving God. He wanted to become God. **We must never desire to become God or to be equal to God.** To do so would be a mistake. God created us and this whole world. God even created Satan. Still, Satan wanted to become God. So God became angry with Satan and forced him out of Heaven. Though Satan was forced out of Heaven, he still has access to God (ref. Job 1:6). Though Satan is against God and all righteousness, it is interesting that he can still come into God's presence and talk to Him and accuse (charge) us of different

[33]

things. Even today, Satan wants to become God and will do anything to take God's place in our lives.

He will do anything within the limits of his power to turn us away from God. We say his power is limited because Satan can only do what God allows him to do. God has supreme power over all things. Satan has mastered the arts of confusion and deception. He uses the things of this world to tempt us to sin because he knows that God hates sin. He will desperately try to confuse us to turn us away from God. We must always be careful and mindful of his presence and his evil ways. The Bible teaches us a lot about him.

****

Learning to be like Jesus will not be easy. As we grow to be like Him, we will face temptations, and we will make mistakes. Mistakes are a part of spiritual growth, so we cannot be too hard on ourselves when we do. God knows the trials and hardships that we face each day. He knows how hard it is to be like Jesus. God made each of us, but as humans, we are not perfect like God. So at times, we will make poor decisions. However, when we make poor decisions, we should learn from them and never repeat them. Learning from our poor decisions is what the Bible means by 'growing in wisdom.'

What is wisdom? **Wisdom** is the ability to make good decisions. It is good, sound judgment and knowing the right thing(s) to do (Wisdom will be discussed in more detail in chapter 7).

We must never yield to the pressures and dares of our friends but always follow and trust God and His

[34]

instructions in the Bible. We must learn to never give in to evil temptations. As we grow to become an adult, we should also grow in wisdom, constantly learning the right things to do. The Bible tells us that if we pray to God and ask Him for wisdom, He will give it to us (James 1:5). The Bible also tells us that there are still things that we must do to receive it (these things are discussed in chapter 7). After receiving wisdom, we still must grow in wisdom. We grow in wisdom by learning from our experiences in life, including our poor decisions, and not repeating them. Also, we grow in wisdom by studying our Bible. Another way that we grow in wisdom is by learning from our parents, teachers, pastors, and elders who have knowledge and wisdom.

Learning is what Jesus loved to do. He loved to learn from His teachers because He knew they had knowledge and wisdom. We can learn many wonderful and important things from our teachers. As a child, this is what Jesus looked forward to and enjoyed. If we want to be just like Jesus, we too must love learning about God from those who know and teach the Bible.

In Jerusalem, there were many wise and knowledgeable teachers who knew a lot about God and His ways. The boy Jesus knew this, and He looked forward to going to Jerusalem to learn from them. So while His family enjoyed the festival, Jesus more enjoyed sitting before the teachers and learning from them. Jesus wanted to know more about God and God's plans for His life. As disciples of Jesus, the more we learn about God, the more we learn about ourselves because God made us in His image (likeness) (Genesis. 1:27).

The teachers were teaching in a large enclosure called the Temple. The Temple had a school that was similar to our seminaries today. A **seminary** is a school or college where pastors, priests, or other people involved in ministry are trained. Smart rabbis enjoyed coming there to teach, and many of them would come from far away and gather there during the Passover festival to share their knowledge. So that is where Jesus went to sit before them and learn from them. This was a wise thing to do and was a good decision. We should always take every opportunity to learn more about God and His kingdom on earth.

Sometimes, while making good decisions, we can also make poor decisions. When the festival ended, and His family left to return to their home in Nazareth, Jesus did not go with them. He remained in Jerusalem, learning from the teachers. One version of the Bible says, *"the child Jesus tarried behind in Jerusalem."* The word **"tarry"** means to stay or remain expecting to receive something. Jesus stayed behind, expecting to receive more blessings from God, more knowledge about God, and a better understanding of Himself and God's purpose for His life. As a rule, we should never be in a hurry when we are learning about God. God is pleased when we give Him our time. He will usually respond by revealing more of Himself to us and revealing more about His will and our purpose in His kingdom. When we tarry before God, we can easily lose awareness of the passing of time as we remain in His presence. Many people who tarry before God will

[36]

say that there is no greater feeling and no greater peace than being in His presence. This often results from tarrying. Perhaps, this is what happened to Jesus. He simply did not realize how much time had passed.

Jesus did not tell His parents or get their permission to remain behind. Therefore, his parents did not know where He was. We must always respect our parents and their authority and love for us by getting their permission to do things that we want to do, even things that they may desire for us to do. Our parents are responsible for our safety and well-being. Our parents may disagree with some of the things we like and desire. As children and youth, we must realize that their disagreements result from the wisdom they have received in life. Our parents have experienced the many things we are now experiencing and can provide us with sound judgments and instructions. We should always respect their judgments and appreciate their concern for us which reflects their love for us.

We should always let them know our plans, where we are going, and who we will be with, so they will not be worried. Sure, many of us desire our privacy and our own space and independence. Many of us desire the freedom to do the things that we like to do, and at the time we want to do them. However, as children and youth, we should always honor and respect our parent's authority and responsibility for us and our well-being. In this instance, Jesus did not do this. On this occasion, remaining behind in Jerusalem without his parent's permission and awareness was the poor decision that Jesus made.

At times, we will make poor decisions. However, in making poor decisions, we never want to sin.

God hates sin, and we must learn to hate what God hates. God loves everybody, but He hates it when we ignore His commandments and commit sinful acts. We should always want to please God. God gave us the Bible so that we will know what He hates and what pleases Him. When we study the Bible, we learn to know what God hates and what pleases Him. So we should study our Bible as much as possible. **As disciples of Jesus, there is no other book that we should study more than the Bible**. This, we should do to be just like Jesus.

As students in school, we have many different classes and many different books that we must study and gain the required knowledge to make passing grades and eventually graduate to the next level. Our books are our learning resources, and we are expected and required to understand the information provided. This is the responsibility placed on us by our schools of higher learning. However, we must prioritize studying the Bible and gaining knowledge of God and His ways above all other knowledge. When we prioritize God above all else, He will open the required doors and give the favor that is needed in all of our other required studies and activities in which we may be involved.

God's **favor** means that He will help us with kind actions according to our needs. **God must always be prioritized above all else to receive His favor.** There is no other knowledge with more meaning in life that will impact our lives more than the knowledge and wisdom gained from studying the Bible, God's holy word.

The Bible tells us that we sin when we disobey our parents. It also tells us that God is pleased when we obey and honor our parents, and we will live a long life on this earth (Eph. 6:3). The Bible informs us that we have all sinned and that Jesus is the only person who has never sinned.

Since disobedience is sin and Jesus is the only person who has never sinned, we know that He did not disobey His parents when He remained in Jerusalem after they had departed to return home. Apparently, His parents never told Him not to go to The Temple. Jesus simply made a poor decision in not informing his parents of where He was and a poor decision in not requesting their permission.

Thankfully, Jesus learned from His mistakes, as we all must learn to do.

Prayer:

Father God, thank You for helping me through all of the poor decisions that I have made. Also, I thank You for all of my teachers, pastors, and elders. Please, bless their efforts in developing the minds of children and youth. I know that they all want to help me grow in knowledge and wisdom, just like Jesus. Please help me to receive the knowledge and understanding that You approve and they desire for me. I ask that You help me to love not just my family, friends, and teachers, but everyone, even those who don't love me, just like Jesus. Amen.

Questions:

1. Define "mistakes."
2. What did you learn about Jesus in this chapter?
3. What is meant by "hostilities of this world?
4. Define "temptation." Can you explain?
5. What does it mean to yield to the temptations of this world? Can you think of some temptations?
6. What are the two parts of the Bible? Define Testament.
7. What are angels? Archangels? What can you tell us about Satan?
8. Why was Satan forced out of Heaven by God? What must we learn from that?
9. What are some of the responsibilities of angels?
10. What is wisdom?
11. What is a seminary?
12. What was the poor decision that Jesus made as a boy? What should He have done differently?
13. What poor decisions have you made that you now know not to repeat? What would you do differently?
14. Explain "God's favor."

Chapter 3

Learning to Listen and Ask Questions

"They found him in the Temple seated among the teachers, listening to them and asking questions."
(The Message Bible) - Luke 2:46

As a twelve-year-old child, Jesus knew the importance of listening and asking questions when He did not understand.

An important part of our Christian growth and development is learning to listen and ask questions. An important part of Godly listening is not so much focused on the brain and what is heard as what the heart understands and how it responds. In other words, the result of listening through the ears and the heart of Jesus is the correct, compassionate response to the needs of all others.

Godly **compassion** is having concern and sympathy for the misfortunes, sufferings, and needs of all others. Compassion is what allows us to walk in the footsteps of others during their time of crisis and feel their pain and hurt as if it were our pain and hurt. As was with Jesus, we must feel the pain and suffering of all others and desire to do all within our power that is legal and moral (unsinful) to give them comfort, aid, and relief.

[41]

In the **kingdom of God** (those who are committed to and living under Christ), when one person is hurting or suffering, everyone is hurting or suffering because of their compassion for the one in need. The compassion and the oneness of God must always be reflected through the life of His servants. His **servants** are His body of believers, those who love Him, commit their lives to Him, and share His love with others. God has always desired that we have the same care and concern for all others that He has for us. Paul said this in his writing in 1st Corinthians 12:26, where he wrote, *"And whether one member suffer, all the members suffer with it; or one member be honoured, all the members rejoice with it"* (KJV).

In listening through the ears and the heart of Jesus, it is not so much as what is actually said by the person in need that is important. It is more important for the hearer to understand what is truly meant and needed for those who are speaking their needs. Many times in the struggles of life, people cannot tell you exactly what they need, simply because many times, people don't truly know what they need. They may feel the hurt and pain resulting from their need, not knowing the actual cause. Most of our needs have an underlying **spiritual** (not physical, things that cannot be seen with the eyes) cause that may not be easily seen or recognized. When we can listen through the heart and ears of Jesus and understand what is meant and needed, we will know the right questions to ask to understand the need better. This will help us determine the correct solution to the real problem causing the pain, suffering, or concern.

A critical requirement for learning to listen with the heart of Jesus is shutting out all surrounding **distractions** (what interrupts or breaks our attention and awareness of God).

Jesus learned the value of listening at an early age. Learning to listen through the heart and ears of Jesus will be much needed as we grow into His image and fulfill our purpose in God's kingdom. The ability to listen with the heart of Jesus will enable us to receive the message(s) of God when He speaks into our hearts or communicates with us by other means and sources.

****

A note of concern: Some may view the following information as being controversial (disputable). However, it is required for fully understanding the Biblically supported methods that God uses to provide revelations that all disciples of Christ must realize.

****

How do we know when God speaks into our hearts? When God **speaks into our heart**, it is a strong feeling that we experience about something or someone, and we instantly know that we must act upon it. God will usually give us an understanding of what we must do when we pray about it and ask Him for understanding and guidance. Usually, we will not have peace or rest until we act upon it according to God's will. Can you recall a time when you had a strong feeling about something or someone and knew that you needed to act upon it? This occurrence could have been God speaking into your heart. We must learn to give attention to those moments.

[43]

Many believers do not believe that God speaks to them personally. Many believe that God only speaks through what is written in the Bible. It is indeed true that God speaks to us through the Bible as we study it. That is why we should constantly study the Bible to receive revelations (something revealed by God) to understand God better and the needs of others.

In addition to speaking to us Person-to-person, God also speaks to us through other people who receive His message(s) and act in obedience as His spokesperson (one who speaks for another) (e.g., 1st Samuel 9:15-10:16, Acts 9:10-19). There are many instances in the Bible where God Personally communicated with humanity or used someone else to communicate for Him. He communicated with Abraham, Moses, Noah, Elijah, Samuel, Paul, and many other people of the Bible. Each of them received, recognized, and responded to His message (revelation) in obedience. Each of them was certain that the message that they received was from God. In speaking to us Person-to-person, God will sometimes use **visions, thoughts**, and in rare cases, **trances** (e.g., Acts 10:10, 22:17) and **audible voices** (e.g., Acts 9:7, 27, 10:13, 15, 11:7, 9). God even opened the mouth of a donkey and enabled her to speak to a human and carry on a conversation (Numbers 22:28).

As just stated, God also speaks to us by placing thoughts in our minds. **Thoughts** (messages) are ideas or information that come into our minds. Earlier, we talked about God speaking into our hearts. Giving us thoughts in our minds is different than speaking into our hearts. Our minds are always busy, and we are

[44]

always thinking. However, we must be very careful when we receive foreign (other than our own) thoughts in our minds. We must never act upon the thoughts in our minds until we verify that they are from God. God does not give us destructive thoughts. He will never tell us to hurt ourselves or someone else. He will never tempt us to sin or do something wrong (not in agreement with the Bible). Only Satan, our enemy, will give us destructive thoughts and tempt us to do wrong. We must always ignore his evil thoughts and messages. God will only give us thoughts that glorify Him, help ourselves, or help somebody else that may be in need. Sometimes, our thought could be a **vision** (picture) of something that we will need to understand (e.g., 2nd Kings 6:17, Daniel 10:7, Acts 9:10, 10:3,11). Most of the time, our thoughts are our own thoughts and are not from God or another source. We verify that they are from God by finding examples of them in the Bible. Then we will know how to respond to them.

If there are no examples in the Bible of the foreign thoughts we receive, we should not accept them or act upon them. If our thoughts do not glorify God, we should ignore them. God is not the only one who will place thoughts in our minds (ref. Matthew 9:4), so we must be very careful how we respond to foreign thoughts that come into our minds. If we receive important thoughts, it is always best to discuss them with our parents or guardians to help us understand them. Also, some thoughts may require their permission before we can act upon them. We must always respect the authority that God has given them.

Finally, as stated, God will also give revelations through trances and audible voices. Though the

[45]

occurrence of these two methods is rare, we must still be mindful of them because they are Biblically supported and are currently experienced by His servants in the twenty-first-century. We must always be mindful of a key Biblical truth. Hebrews 13:8 states, *"Jesus Christ is the same yesterday, today, and forever."* This verse means that Jesus Christ does not change. What He did in the past, He will do today and always. This verse also applies to communication.

A **trance** is a semiconscious state, as between sleeping and waking. It may be understood as being in a daze. In this state of being arranged by God, He will give revelation (e.g., Acts 10:10-16, 22:17-21).

An **audible voice** is an actual voice from Heaven that will be heard with our ears (e.g., Acts 9:7, 27, 10:13, 15, 11:7, 9).

Finally, it is always good to pray to our heavenly Father for Him to help us to understand the messages (revelations) that we receive. Again, the best way to listen to God is by studying the Bible.

****

As stated, there are many examples in the Bible of God communicating with His servants.

Noah knew to build the ark that saved his immediate family and two of each kind of animal on the earth during the great flood because he received a revelation and instructions from God (Genesis 6:13).

Abraham knew to leave his home and family to travel to a new land because he received a revelation and instructions from God (Genesis 12:1-3).

The apostle Paul was able to write all of his writings in the New Testament because he received revelations from God, which gave him the information to write. Noah, Abraham, Paul, and the others that we have mentioned were able to receive God's message(s) and accomplish God's will for their lives. God had something special that He wanted each of them to do in His kingdom here on earth just as He has for all of His servants.

Just like all of them, we too can receive God's revelations and accomplish His will for our lives. The author of this book knew to write it because God revealed His instructions into his heart. Just like each of these mentioned, God has something special for each of us to do in His kingdom here on earth. But we must be able to listen and receive His message(s) when He speaks. Then, we must distinguish (tell the difference, to know) God's message(s) when He speaks.

God is not the only one who speaks to us through other people and into our hearts and minds. Sometimes we can receive other revelations and messages that may appear to be from God but may not be from Him. Our enemy, Satan, can also speak to us through other people and into our hearts and minds and pretend to be God. He is a great **deceiver** (one who causes you to believe something that is not true). He will speak to us to deceive us and cause us to do things that God does not will for us to do. As children and youth of God, we must be cautious about who and what we listen to and expose ourselves.

If we listen to ungodly things and expose ourselves to ungodly things, then we make it easy for Satan to speak into our hearts and minds, confuse us, and give us ideas that God does not desire for us. When we listen to ungodly music, watch ungodly movies and videos, play ungodly games, entertain ungodly conversation with our friends, or entertain ungodly things on television or social media, we allow Satan to speak to us and convince us to do things against God's will. These are just some of the things of this world that Satan will use against us. He knows that these are things of the world that we enjoy. That is why God says that worldly people are His enemies (James 4:4). When we allow the evil things of this world to enter into our minds and hearts and change who we are or who we should become in God's kingdom, we become an enemy of God. God instructs us to **submit** (stop fighting against Him, give in) ourselves to Him, **resist** (fight off, stand against) Satan, and he will run away from us (James 4:7). We resist Satan by not listening to or exposing ourselves to the ungodly things of this world, dedicating ourselves to prayer to our heavenly Father, and studying the Bible as our main book in life.

How do we know that the message we receive is from God? God's message will always agree with what is written about Him in the Bible. When we receive a message from God or a revelation in our hearts (a strong feeling that we experience about something or someone, and we instantly know that we must act upon it), we should always search the Bible to find an example of what we have received and how we should respond. Many times the Bible will give us a better understanding of the message we receive. This is the best way to be sure that the message(s) we receive is from God. Also, God's message(s) will always glorify Him and His kingdom.

Glorify, as used here, means that the message we receive will honor, exalt and hold God in high regard and benefit His kingdom and those who trust Him. Also, His message(s) will often give us instructions for speaking to and dealing with others in our life with words and actions of love. As God's servants, we want everyone to know Him, trust Him, place their lives in His care, and receive His **eternal salvation** (forgiveness of their sins, knowing God, and living with Him forever).

Remember, God is love, and all of His messages to us will reflect His love and the concerns of His kingdom.

Our enemy, Satan, knows this and desires that we never receive God's messages. He never wants us to receive what God is saying to us so that he can keep us in a state of confusion. Satan desires that we not receive God's warnings and instructions and not realize the appropriate course of action in our lives when needed.

Satan will use different things of this world to distract our attention away from God. One distraction that often results from worldliness (entertaining the things of this world) is **ungodly noise,** usually as music. **All music that we listen to or sing must glorify God as acts of worship, never the evilness of this world**. Noise will distract us and keep us from receiving the revelation(s) of God when He communicates with us. Therefore, we must shut out the confusions of worldliness, which often results from the

[49]

distraction of noise that enters our ears and remains in our hearts. As worldly confusion remains in our hearts, we cannot receive God's revelations. Also, we must shut out the **visions of worldliness** that enter our eyes and remain in our hearts. We must be careful in what we allow ourselves to hear and what we allow ourselves to see.

The two most common sources for these distractions in America are television and social media. Americans watch television more than any other country in the world (Americans watch TV an average of 28 hours/week and spend an average of 15 hours/week on social media). **Christian disciples must avoid the worldliness of television and social media.**

It is common in today's culture for children and youth to fill their environments with some form of ungodly noise, ungodly games, or ungodly videos. Many of us find entertainment and satisfaction through some form of worldly-focused noise, games, or videos, not realizing that God may need to get our attention for a much-needed purpose. It is always God's desire that we do not suffer and make wrong decisions in life. Many times He will want to speak urgent words of instruction, correction, or warning to us. So, as a maturing child or youth who wants to be like Jesus, we must learn to prioritize (set aside as more important) our times of silence when we can receive God's revelations. We must remove ourselves from the distractions of worldliness, both sound (what we hear) and vision (what we allow ourselves to see).

Like the boy Jesus, we must learn how to tarry (sitting patiently, expecting to receive) before the Lord and listen in our hearts for His revelations. God will often speak when we are not focused on listening for Him. So, we must at all times remain focused on listening and receiving from Him as a way of life, even while we are busy doing other things.

****

As a child, Jesus knew the value of God-focused listening. When it was realized that Jesus was not in the caravan returning from Jerusalem, His mother, Mary, and His father Joseph returned to Jerusalem to find Him. It is interesting to note that they did not find Him in the normally expected places that a child would often be found. He was not found on the main streets of Jerusalem listening to, watching, and being entertained by the sights and the sounds of worldliness. He was not found listening to the ungodly music of those who provided entertainment along the busy streets of Jerusalem or watching those who entertained for money. Usually, children and youth are attracted to the noise and excitement of worldliness. This environment would have perhaps been the usual place to look for a missing child. However, Jesus was not found where one would typically expect to find a twelve-year-old child.

Luke 2:46 informs us, *"The next day they found him in the Temple seated among the teachers, listening to them and asking questions"* (Message Bible). The Temple was an unexpected place to find a twelve-year-old child who was not forced or pressured to be there. Usually, children and youth are encouraged by parents and guardians to spend time in the presence of God, mainly by attending church or church-related

[51]

activities. Jesus had his choices of places to go and things to see and do because his parents were not there to tell him differently.

As children and youth of God, we must always be like Jesus and do only the things that please God, even when no one else sees us or knows about it. God sees everything that we see and do. He hears everything that we hear and say. He knows the thoughts of our minds and the desires of our hearts. There is nothing about us that is hidden from God. Jesus wanted His disciples to be mindful of this truth about God when He said to them in Luke 8:16-17, *"For nothing is secret that will not be revealed, nor anything hidden that will not be known and come to light. Therefore take heed how you hear"* (NKJV) (also, Luke 12:2-3). We will be rewarded by God for the things that we do in secret that honor God and reveal our obedience and love for Him (Matthew 6:6).

Indeed, Jesus was not an average child. Sure, He was the Son of God, but He was as human as you and I. He was born to a human mother (Matt. 1:25). He faced the same temptations, and the same trials as you and I face (Heb. 4:15). He felt the same hurt and pain that we feel (Matt. 16:21). He experienced the same disappointments in life that we experience. He had the same needs that we all have. He experienced hunger as you and I do (Matt. 21:18). He valued the friendship and love of others like you, and I do (Jn. 11:5).

He was different because He loved His Father in Heaven more than He loved anyone or anything else on this earth. Sure, He loved His mother Mary, His father Joseph, and His brothers and sisters, but He loved His heavenly Father more. He was also different because He knew and valued the love of His Father in Heaven. He truly wanted to please His heavenly Father (John 8:29). He also knew that He had a purpose on earth that was given to Him by His heavenly Father. His priority in life was to fully understand and complete His purpose, His heavenly Father's will.

Today, most children and youth do not realize that God has given them a purpose in His kingdom on earth, just as He gave Jesus a purpose. So, many of them find purpose in doing things that God does not will for them to do. It is an honor to know that God has given each of us a purpose in His kingdom, something that is important that He prepares us and trusts us to do. There is something that God has purposed for us that is unique (only) for us. To realize our purpose, we must be able to receive God's message(s) when He speaks to us. Many of today's children and youth do not know their purpose in God's kingdom because they have worldly distractions in their lives that shut out all revelations from God. They are primarily attracted to the things of this evil world than the things of God.

The Bible tells us a lot about God and His kingdom, but it does not reveal our individual, unique purpose in His kingdom. As children and youth of Christ, we must shut out the worldly noise and distractions of life and learn to listen with our hearts for God's revelations. Rather than following the distractions and temptations of worldliness, Jesus remained focused on His purpose in God's kingdom and receiving God's instructions for His life. As a child, Jesus valued every opportunity when He could listen, learn, ask, and receive answers to

His questions about His heavenly Father and His kingdom on earth.

It is also important to note that Jesus would ask questions when He did not understand something. Effective God-focused listening will always result in knowing the correct questions to ask. It shows great respect to someone and makes them feel appreciated when they see that we really listen to them and are interested in learning what they are teaching us. The questions that we ask will reveal our interest in what they are teaching. Many times we will ask questions for the wrong reasons.

Some of us will ask questions hoping to be seen as showing interest in the discussed topic. However, we may not be aware that the nature of our questions will often reveal our level or lack of interest. Some questions will often be asked with the hope of impressing others with our great knowledge of the discussed topic. Many of today's children and youth do not ask questions, even when they do not understand. They may not want others to know how little they know and may feel a sense of embarrassment (feeling self-conscience, shame). Many of today's children and youth will yield to the pressure and desire to maintain their friends' approval and acceptance, than obeying, honoring, and learning about God. These motivations for asking or not asking questions must never be a part of a God-focused, caring, and learning environment. As disciples of Christ, we can never allow these reasons for asking or not asking questions to become a part of our character. Our primary focus must always be on learning as much as we can, in every opportunity we receive, even in an uncaring and perhaps ungodly environment. Even in an uncaring and ungodly environment, we can learn how **not** to think and act.

We must never be fearful of asking questions when we need to understand better. However, we must ultimately only receive and accept the things of this world that truly glorify and honor God. God and His kingdom must remain our main interest in life.

To be like Jesus, we must learn to listen, not just with our minds but with our hearts, ask questions when we do not understand, and have compassion for the needs of all others when needed.

Prayer:

Father God, thank You for showing me how to listen, just like Jesus. I now realize that listening with the heart of Jesus is not so much as what I hear in my ears as what I receive and understand in my heart. Help me to show compassion to all others when needed. I ask that You shelter me from worldly distractions so that I may hear You when You speak. Enable me to know when you are speaking and enable me to receive and honor Your messages. I want to fulfill my purpose in Your kingdom, but I need Your help to do so. Speak into my heart Your purpose for my life and your will for every occasion. For the glory of Your kingdom, I ask. Amen.

Questions:

1. What is the meaning of compassion?
2. What is meant by "the kingdom of God?"
3. What does it mean to listen with the heart of Jesus?
4. Why must we learn to listen with the heart of Jesus?
5. How do we know when God speaks into our hearts?
6. Name the different ways that God communicates with us. Can you explain them?
7. How do we know the message we receive is from God?
8. Why must we avoid worldly distractions in life?
9. List some distractions for receiving revelations from God.
10. What are the two most common distractions in America for receiving revelations from God? Can you explain? What could we do instead?
11. How many worldly distractions can you list that you are currently experiencing in your life?
12. What is meant by "Satan is a great deceiver?"
13. Why does Satan not want us to receive revelations from God?
14. Where did Jesus' parents find Him in Jerusalem? Why was He there?
15. What does it mean to have a purpose in life?
16. How do you feel about asking questions in the classroom or Bible study when you don't understand something?

Chapter 4

Studying to Gain Understanding

"And all that heard him were astonished at his understanding and answers" (KJV). - Luke 2:47

In chapter three, we talked about the importance of learning to listen and asking questions. These two important disciplines are required for Christian growth and development. In this chapter, we will look at the need to understand what we learn and how our understanding of what we learn affects the answers we give when asked questions.

As a child, Jesus gave good answers to His teacher's questions based on His understanding.

Everyone in this world will need answers to questions about their life at some point in their lifetime. As we live, we will have many problems in our lives. Problems occur in every area of life, which will always be so. New problems happen daily and often at a faster rate than we can provide answers. Answers will even be required to sustain life. Problems that are presently developing in science now have scientists working every day to produce answers and solutions. During the writing of this book, there is a pandemic (COVID-19) that is taking many human lives worldwide. Scientists and world leaders are working very hard to develop answers and solutions to end this global problem.

During this same time, America and many other parts of the world are dealing with problems in race relations, wealth inequality, injustice, poverty, voter suppression (maintaining inequality and injustice by making it harder for those who are oppressed to vote), confusion in religion, and sin in general. These problems reflect the growing hatred and lack of love among humans of different races, backgrounds, and cultures worldwide. Conflicts and worldwide fighting are increasing, such as in Afghanistan and the ongoing Israeli–Palestinian conflict in the Middle East. These conflicts are proving to be two of the world's most long-lasting. Disputes between different people and groups are happening worldwide, and there seem to be no worldly answers or solutions to end them. Each side in these conflicts is asking for something that the other side will never agree to give. World leaders are unable to provide acceptable answers to resolve these conflicts. Many innocent people are trapped in the middle of these conflicts and wars and are losing their possessions, their homes, and even their lives as a result. Many people around the world live each day in pain and suffering caused by war and poverty. Worldwide aggression (hostile or violent behavior toward someone else) usually results from the sin of **greed** (a selfish desire for something, taking all that one can get) that reflects the human desire for more power, more wealth, and more control. On a worldwide scale, no one wants to give or sacrifice anything to what is often viewed as the opposition (enemy). Everyone is seemingly looking for answers for the

[58]

many problems throughout this world, but very few answers are found.

When we review the ongoing problems of this world using the Bible as our guide for solving problems, we can easily see something important. **An example of all of the problems of this world can be found in the Bible.** All of the problems we hear about today have happened before in world history and are discussed in our Bible. Ecclesiastes 1:9 states, *"History merely repeats itself. Nothing is truly new; it has all been done or said before."* The same answers that solved them in the Bible are the same answers that will end them today. The solutions that are in the Bible will only be seen by God's servants, those who study and understand the Bible and receive God's revelations. The more we study the Bible, the better we will understand its answers. Every child and youth of Christ must pray to God for His help before studying the Bible in order to get His understanding. Because all of the answers to life problems are found in the Bible, this makes the Bible the required research and resource book for solving world problems. Many of the answers for the problems of this world are found in the book of Proverbs.

Because the boy Jesus loved to study about God, He was able to give good answers about God's kingdom. Just like Jesus, when we study about God, we too will be able to provide good answers about God and His kingdom to everyone who needs to know about Him and His kingdom order.

With the growing number of problems throughout the world and very few answers realized, what can we learn from Jesus at the tender age of twelve years old that will help the world today? What can our children and youth learn about Him that will help them give good answers and solve large problems?

Luke 2:47 states, *"And all that heard him were astonished at his understanding and answers"* (KJV). This simply means that the teachers and everyone else were incredibly impressed and amazed at Jesus's answers to their questions. They did not expect this level of understanding from a child at the age of twelve years old. Apparently, Jesus provided great answers to difficult questions. We are not told the specific questions to which Jesus provided answers. However, we know that His answers were related to God's kingdom because this was the focus of the rabbi teachings in the Temple school. The Bible does not give information about Jesus' secular (non-religious) education or His interest in non-religious schools. However, we can easily see His great interest in understanding Bible matters and the kingdom of God. He had great interest and spent much time learning about His heavenly Father, His Father's kingdom on earth, and His Father's will for His life.

As children and youth of God, we must begin to prioritize the childhood interest of Jesus as our interest and see Jesus as our model for studying about God if we want to be just like Him. Even as a child, His primary interest was to better understand the kingdom of God above everything else in His life. His understanding of God's kingdom was seen in the good answers to His teachers (rabbis). **We can only give good answers when we study and understand what**

we are studying. **Our answers on a given topic reflect the amount of time spent studying that topic.** When we study and understand the Bible, we will be able to give good answers to life's concerns and this world's problems. Our religious leaders and world leaders can learn a lot from the boy Jesus about getting solutions for the issues of life and this world. The Bible must become our primary tool for research and our resource for all problems in life.

The answers to this world's growing list of difficult problems and concerns can be realized and better understood when viewed through Bible history. The Bible reveals the reason for all of the problems of this world. **The problems exist because the world has turned away from God and ignores His requirements for abundant life and peace.** Unlike the kingdom of God, the world is not guided by the word of God and is not led by the Spirit of God. As a result, we now live in a world that reflects all the signs of godlessness (existing without God's oversight). As to be expected, the world is characterized by ever-increasing conflicts and many other signs that reflect Satan's involvement and the absence of the oversight, guidance, and protection of God.

Many people are praying to God for Him to end the many frightening (scary) concerns of this world. Some are asking, "Where is God?" Many nonbelievers are questioning if God even exists because of the pain, suffering, increasing ungodliness throughout the world, and the diminishing number of committed followers of Christ in America and Western Europe. The human forces of the righteousness of Christ are on the decline.

[61]

****

As a sidetrack but important note, the title **"Christ"** was not the actual name of Jesus. It was a title given to Jesus because it means "the anointed one." A person who is **anointed** is empowered by God to carry out a specific task. Because God calls (selects) them, He prepares them and gives them what they will need. Jesus was given power from God that proved to the world who he really was, the anointed of God. Jesus was referred to as Jesus, the Christ. Jesus' name in Hebrew is **"Yeshua."**

****

As believers in Christ, there are lasting Biblical facts that we must always believe. We know from the Bible that God created this world and made man in His image (Genesis 1:1, 27). We also know from the Bible that God has all power **(omnipotent)**, and His knowledge can't be measured because God knows everything **(omniscient)** (Psalm 147:5). Since we know that God created this world and humanity and has all knowledge and power, we can say for sure that God has all of the answers to His world's concerns. There is nothing in this world of which God is not fully aware or unable to change or resolve. God can make all things new (Rev. 21:5).

Our scripture for this chapter about the boy Jesus reminds us of two Biblical facts for problem resolution that the religious leaders of this world must understand.

Determining the answers for this world's problems is directly related to our understanding of the real causes. Our focus for resolution is often on the **symptom** (a sign of the presence of something) and not the real cause of the problem. The boy Jesus's impressive answers given to His teachers resulted from His level of understanding of what they were discussing. Understanding Biblical matters begins with a commitment to seeking God with all of our heart, soul, mind, and strength. This level of commitment dedicates everything about us to that end desire, especially our time. As children and youth who want to be just like Jesus, we must learn to spend time with God by tarrying before Him, studying the Bible, praying to Him, and listening for His revelations.

The boy Jesus did not receive His great level of understanding at this one meeting with the rabbis. His understanding resulted from a committed life to learning about God and His kingdom plan and order. As earlier stated, even at the tender age of twelve years old, Jesus was committed to that purpose. He was committed to understanding all that He could about God's kingdom. This level of commitment prioritizes this one desire above all else in our lives. Sure, we are to receive a non-religious education in our school systems and homeschools. But our Biblical education must be our number one priority in life to which we must remain committed (John 15:4,7). We must not allow any other education to become more important to us as disciples of Jesus. Being committed implies a desire to remain in the word of God, a commitment to obedience, and constantly seeking the will of God for our lives. These must be guided and reinforced by a life-focus of faith and prayer to our heavenly Father. Once we gain a Biblical understanding of God's kingdom order, like the boy Jesus, our answers to the concerns of life will be realized and appreciated by all others. Not only will God be glorified, but He will reward our effort.

Let us leave this point, for now, to look at another point regarding Biblical solutions for world problems.

There is an important scripture in the Old Testament that is required for this particular discussion. In the 7th chapter of the 2nd Chronicles, we read God's response to King Solomon's request made in the 6th chapter. King Solomon requested that God would provide a means for restoring the Israelites when they had sinned and turned from Him. God gave the requirements of His plan in chapter 7, verse 14. God said to King Solomon, *"If my people, which are called by my name, shall <u>humble themselves</u>, and <u>pray</u>, and <u>seek my face</u>, and <u>turn from their wicked ways</u>; then will I hear from heaven, and will forgive their sin, and will heal their land"* (KJV). Though this was God's response to King Solomon's request for the Israelites, Bible teachers have said that these four conditions were given and meant to remain forever for all people of God. These four conditions remain God's requirements for restoring our relationship with Him after sinful separations from Him. This is a familiar scripture to most believers. Its importance must never be overlooked.

God was referring to the Israelites when he said, *"If my people."* These were the focused people for God's restoration. His chosen people during that time were the people of Israel. However, today all believers are God's people. If you commit your life to God by accepting Jesus as your Lord and Savior and live a life of faith, love, holiness, and obedience, then you are a part of God's people today. So these four things that God said to Solomon apply to you and everyone else who accepts Jesus as their Lord and Savior. When we review these requirements of God for restoration, it is important to point out two things.

First, these requirements are only given to God's people, His servants. God begins these requirements by making this known. It is important to understand that the restoration of this world to Him is not based on the world's ability to change or the world's relationship to Him. It is solely based on His servant's relationship to Him. The solutions for this world's problems are really in the hands of the professing body of Christ and are based on their relationship to God.

Second, God gave four requirements that His servants must honor for restoration. As a church body, we must humble ourselves (willing to admit that we were wrong) and pray to God. We must seek God's face (seek His presence through prayer) and turn from our sins in repentance. **Repentance** (sorrow, regret) implies not just turning from sin but fully turning to God. These are God's requirements for restoration and His solution to the problems of His creation. How sincere we are in doing this will determine the outcome. God stated that when these conditions are met, He will heal our land. This almost sounds too simple to believe. The seemingly difficult solutions to this world's problems are not possible through any of the worldly efforts of this ungodly world. The world and its leadership do not have a **covenant** (an agreement that cannot be broken) relationship with God and have no knowledge or understanding of Biblical and spiritual matters. It is unable to receive God's revelations. God's people, the believers of today, hold the key to solving all of the problems of God's creation because all of the problems have a spiritual origin (Eph. 6:12). Our enemy Satan has realized this fact throughout the ages. He has developed effective strategies against the professing church of God to keep this world in bondage, in a state of confusion, and under his control.

Primarily, the professing church of God in America has embraced worldliness, resulting in its separation from God (James 4:4). It has yielded to Satan's strategies to destroy the foundation that God gave for His kingdom. God's foundation from the very beginning required that His servants have total faith, obedience, and sacrificial and unconditional love for Him and all others.

Sacrificial love means giving up something that is very special to you to help others.

Unconditional love is love given without strings attached. It is freely given. It is not based on what someone does for you in return.

God's church has not successfully resisted Satan's strategies throughout the ages, and God's required foundation for His kingdom has eroded (slowly destroyed). Faith, obedience, and unconditional, sacrificial love for God and all others is no longer prioritized in the modern-day professing church of God to the joy and delight of Satan and his forces of evil. Not only is this required foundation not modeled by many people who say that they love God, but some also

[66]

see it as impossible and an unrealistic goal. Therefore, it is not seriously considered as being required for change. This required foundational structure is not even a focus of discussion among the current spiritual leadership. The professing church of God has truly lost its required Biblical character. By all means, the professing church of God must restore its required foundation and honor the four requirements of God for restoration with a whole-hearted effort. This effort will enable the world to receive the much-needed answers for its problems and long-overdue healing that only can come from God.

After carefully reviewing the present condition and confusion of the modern-day church and the unlikelihood of serious and lasting change, it is now required that the children and youth of our world take it upon themselves to be just like Jesus. In so doing, assume the responsibility of restoring Jesus' church to its original Biblical design of faith, obedience to God, and unconditional, sacrificial love for God and all others. Because of unsuccessful efforts by adults, children and youth must now take an active role in leading the way back to Christ to restore the required leadership of the Spirit of God.

To be just like Jesus and change the world, children and youth must commit themselves to studying the Bible to gain God's understanding in all matters of life. This commitment will help them receive God's answers to their concerns and the concerns of this world. This effort by children and youth must be strengthened by continuous prayer (1st Thess. 5:17).

Prayer:

Heavenly Father, I thank You for the revelations from the early life of Your Son Jesus. I ask that You give me His same hunger to understand Your Biblical applications to life as revealed in Your holy word and understand Your kingdom on earth. I ask this so that I, like Jesus, will have the necessary answers to kingdom and world concerns. In Jesus' name, I pray. Amen.

Questions:

1. What is the meaning of "greed?"
2. What is a "rabbi?" What did they teach?
3. Why were the rabbis impressed with the boy Jesus?
4. What was it about Jesus that enabled Him to give good answers?
5. What is the meaning of "Christ?"
6. What was Jesus' name in Hebrew?
7. What does it mean to be "anointed?" Explain.
8. What is meant by God is omnipotent? Omniscient?
9. What is meant by "a symptom of the problem?"
10. What are the four requirements of God for His intervention into our problems?
11. What is the meaning of "repentance?"
12. What is a "covenant?"
13. Can you explain God's foundation for this world?
14. What is sacrificial love? Unconditional love?

Chapter 5

Our Heavenly Father's Business

"Did you not know that I must be about My Father's business?" (NKJV) - Luke 2:49

As a child, Jesus not only knew that there was something that His heavenly Father wanted Him to do for His kingdom, He also knew that His heavenly Father's business was important.

Every child and youth should see themselves as Jesus saw himself when He was a child. Every child and youth should see themselves as having a purpose in life that God has given them. They should all feel that their purpose is important and something to be prioritized and desired above all else. Though they may not know what that purpose is, they should not be discouraged because of that. Like the boy Jesus, they should want to spend as much time with God as possible, studying and praying to Him for understanding and asking Him to show them His purpose for their life. God has given everyone on earth a purpose for their life in His kingdom.

We should see ourselves as one piece of a giant puzzle (the different pictures of the kingdom of God on earth). Everyone who has put a puzzle together knows how important each piece is to the finished picture. We see how the finished picture is supposed to look on the front of the box that contains the unassembled pieces of the puzzle. For God's kingdom, the front of the box is the Bible. When we study and understand the Bible, we will see how the kingdom of God is supposed to look when all of the pieces are in their proper place and correctly positioned. If one piece is missing or not in the correct position, the puzzle is incomplete and does not look presentable. The picture will not look complete until every piece is positioned correctly in its required place. When in its correct place, each piece cannot see how the finished picture looks; only God can. When God sees every piece in its proper place and positioned correctly, He sees the whole finished picture and is pleased. He enjoys looking at the picture that He has put together, and every piece of the puzzle is special to Him. All of the pieces are important to the completed picture. They may be different in size, position, and location on the puzzle, but all of them are just as important as the other pieces. Just like the pieces of a puzzle, we all are different. We may have different features. We may be different in color and size. In size, we may be big or small. But to God, we all look perfect because He made us, and He loves each of us the same, and each of us is important to Him. This is how God's kingdom looks to Him.

If every person whom He has assigned a position in His kingdom is not in their proper place, then His kingdom is incomplete and will not look as He wants it to look. Every person's purpose looks different from everyone else's. However, when each piece is in its correct place and positioned correctly, the picture is complete, looks beautiful, and glorifies God, its maker.

****

What does it mean to glorify God? **Glorifying God** means that we act in ways that look like Him and bring attention to how great He really is. It means that we see our lives as shining a light on God through how we live so everyone else can see Him better by looking at Him through our light. How we live our lives is the light that we shine on the world. When they can see Him better through our light, how caring and wonderful He really is, they will want to know Him and be with Him forever.

This is called evangelism. **Evangelism** is telling others about Jesus and sharing the good news of His love and salvation. God wants all of His servants to tell others about Jesus and why He sent Him to the earth. We best tell others about Jesus as we live like Jesus.

****

Just like Jesus, children and youth should not prioritize the choices in life that will get them the most money, fame, worldly pleasures, and things of life. This life priority is the way of the world. Instead, they should prioritize the choices that will give God the most glory throughout their life. This unselfish focus for life will help lead them to God's purpose for their life. This priority applies to every area of life, especially their jobs and career choices. They should view their career choices through the sacrificial eyes and mindset of Jesus. They should see their career choices as 'stepping stones' and means of positioning themselves to receive God's will for their life. Though children and youth may not yet know God's will for their life, they should know what glorifies God in all of their choices in life. The Bible should remain our resource for all of our decisions in life. When glorifying God becomes the focus for their life, God will give His favor and required guidance for their life choices.

Before making decisions in life, they should always seek God's direction through prayer. Prayer should remain the God-given tool for clarity of life and should be used without ceasing (1st Thessalonians 5:17).

All too often, adults realize later in life the errors of many of their youthful choices and decisions, and with regret, wish they had done things differently. The primary reason for many of their regretful and life-altering mistakes in life is that they did not honor God's kingdom order for life. They failed to first seek God's kingdom (His will) and His righteousness before making other major decisions regarding their lives.

Many of the choices that children and youth make in life do not focus on glorifying God but on obtaining the things of this world. This common mistake can easily be avoided when we choose to live our lives according to God's Divine order. God desires that we not make regretful decisions and choices in life.

God gave all of His servants a simple command to honor before making any decisions about life and its

[72]

required provisions. He stated in Matthew 6:33, ***"But seek ye first the kingdom of God, and his righteousness; and all these things shall be added unto you*** (KJV).*"* When we obey this command of God, the things that will be added to us are all of the things that we need in life to physically exist, be prosperous (fulfilling the sacrificial, God-ordained will for our lives), and live in perfect harmony with God.

In its commentary on this scripture, The Life Application Study Bible states, "To seek 'first the kingdom of God, and his righteousness' means to turn to him first for help, to fill your thoughts with his desires, to take his character for your pattern, and to serve and obey him in everything   What is really important to you?   People, objects, goals, and other desires all compete for priority.   Any of these can quickly bump God out of first place if you don't actively choose to give him first place in every area of your life."   As a result of this common error, many regretful decisions and choices about life are needlessly made and later realized.   Again, God desires that we not make regretful decisions and choices in life.

When we prioritize God's will for our life or our position in the 'puzzles of His kingdom' (our earlier used analogy), He will honor our commitment with His presence and guidance in life.   Through His presence, we will experience 'real' joy in life (ref. Psalm 16:11).

****

We don't know how old Jesus was when He first knew His heavenly Father's will for His life.   However, as a boy, Jesus saw Himself as one placed on the earth to complete His heavenly Father's will. Not only did Jesus understand this Himself, but He also wanted everyone else, including His parents, to be mindful of that fact. So when his mother and father found Him in the Temple and questioned Him about it, he asked them, *"Why is it that you sought Me? Did you not know that I must be about My Father's business?"* Jesus wanted His parents and everyone else to understand His life as one on an assignment for his heavenly Father. Just like Jesus, we should want everyone to understand our lives as one on a mission for our heavenly Father. When people see you as an image of Christ in God's kingdom, many of them will want to help you in any way that they can. They will see you as different from other children and youth and view you as a model they hope all children and youth will follow. As we said, just like Jesus, we should see ourselves as having a God-given purpose that we must fulfill. As we grow and mature, all of our interests should reflect that desire. Our purpose in life should be understood as the will of God for our lives.

After Jesus's parents found Him in the Temple, His mother Mary angrily said to Him. *"Your father and I have been frantic, searching for you everywhere"* (Luke 2:48). He asked them, *"But why did you need to search"* (Luke 2:49)? In other words, Jesus was asking them, "Why would you look for me any other place?" Jesus implied that they should have known that the Temple would be the first place to look for Him. The Bible tells us that Mary and Joseph looked a whole

[74]

day for Jesus. The fact that they spent an entire day looking for Him implied that they looked in other places before they found Him in the Temple.

Jesus asked them, *"Didn't you realize that I would be here at the Temple, in my Father's House?"* His Father's business was His primary interest in life. So the Temple should have been the first place that His parents looked for Him. If you were missing, what would be the first place that your parents would look for you based on your interest in life?

When Jesus asked, *"Did you not know"* (NKJV), this phrase meant that Jesus expected them to know that His heavenly Father's business was His priority in life. For Jesus to have expected His parents to know implied that He had given them every reason to know His life priority. For Jesus, this was His main interest. To Jesus, they should have known because they were his parents and had observed His interest throughout His childhood (Luke 2:40). So, understandably, Jesus was surprised that His parents did not know His primary interest in life. As a child, Jesus' whole interest was taken up with knowing and fulfilling His heavenly Father's will for His life.

What about you? Is your interest taken up with knowing and fulfilling your heavenly Father's will for your life? Do your parents know your primary interest in life? From the interest you show as you live, would your parents and friends see any interest in Jesus? Would they be surprised to know that you are interested in Jesus and God's will for your life?

[75]

****

God has given each person in His kingdom two types of wills for their life on earth. Each person has a **corporate will** for their life, and each person has what we will call a **distinct, personal will** for their life. God's wills for our lives are what He desires from us as we commit our lives to Him and live for Him.

Corporate means everyone. God's corporate will is the same for each of us on the earth. God's corporate will is that we **believe in Christ**. His corporate will is that we **do not sin**. However, if we sin, His corporate will is that we **repent of our sins and live a holy life** (ref. Matthew 5:48, 1st Peter 1:14-16, Hebrews 12:14). [(**"Holy"** means the character or image of God. To live a holy life means you want to be pure and free from sin. It means that you are living as Jesus lived) **(As earlier stated, we must live holy lives, but we must never desire to become God or equal to Him)**]. God's corporate will is that we **love Him with all of our heart, soul, mind, and strength** and that we **love all others as we love ourselves**. His corporate will is that we **obey and honor Him and our parents and guardians**. We all are required to honor God's corporate will so that we can live forever with Him in Heaven. When we honor God's corporate will, it shows Him that we believe in Jesus and trust (have faith in) Him.

Also, each person who is a servant of God has a distinct, personal will that God wants them to honor and fulfill. God's **distinct, personal will** is something that God desires from them individually as they live for

[76]

Him. They may be the only ones to do what God desires of them individually. However, there may also be others who are given this same responsibility, but it is not the same for everyone in His kingdom. Regretfully, most believers do not know God's distinct, personal will for their lives. However, it is God's desire for everyone to know His distinct, personal will for their lives.

There are many examples in the Bible of individuals receiving, honoring, and fulfilling God's distinct, personal will for their lives. The Bible gives us these examples so that we can see and believe that it is truly God's desire for us to know His distinct, personal will also. God also wants us to use their examples of radical (very great) obedience to Him as our models in life.

One individual from the Bible was Noah. God's distinct, personal will for Noah was for him to build an ark (a large vessel that floats on water) for Noah and his family and two animals of each kind. The ark was required to survive the flood that God was sending to destroy all life on the earth because of sin (Genesis 6). God did not will for anyone else on the earth to build an ark, only Noah.

Another individual from the Bible was Moses. God's distinct, personal will for Moses was for him to gain the freedom of the Israelites from slavery and to lead them from Egypt to Canaan, a land that God was giving them. The Israelites were enslaved in Egypt, and God decided to use Moses to gain their freedom and lead them to their new home (Exodus 3).

Two other examples from the Bible are Saul and David. God chose Saul to be the first king of Israel. This was God's distinct, personal will for Saul. However, as king, Saul disobeyed God, and as a result, God no longer wanted Saul to be the king. We must be very careful to obey God when He gives us His distinct, personal will for our lives. God does not like it when we rebel against His will. As the result of Saul's disobedience, God chose David to replace Saul as Israel's new king. So God's distinct, personal will for David was to become the new king of Israel (1st Samuel 16).

Our final example from the Bible is Mary, the mother of Jesus. God chose Mary to be the earthly mother of Jesus, to birth Him and to care for Him. This was God's distinct, personal will for Mary (Luke 1). [(An important point to remember about Mary is that she was as human as us all. Although God chose her to be the mother of Jesus, she was not Divine (like God), therefore, we must not pray to her or worship her. As earlier stated, worship for believers is showing ultimate devotion, honor, and respect for God only)].

****

In reviewing these examples from the Bible, there is one thing that we must be mindful of, as seen in the example of Saul. God chose Saul to become Israel's first king. This was God's distinct, personal will for Saul's life. Regretfully, while serving as king, Saul

[78]

disobeyed God. Because of his disobedience, God became angry with him and decided to replace him as Israel's king.

When we look back at the completed picture from our puzzle, we can better understand what God sees. As we said, each piece of the puzzle is needed to complete the picture. Because God made the puzzle, if one piece is damaged or missing, He will make another piece as a substitute (use in its place). God will not allow a single piece of the puzzle to stop its completion. It is always God's desire that His puzzle is complete with every piece in its correct place and properly positioned.

Many people have found their correct place (God's distinct, personal will for their lives) in God's kingdom but are not properly positioned. They are not properly positioned if they do not have the mind of Christ or the heart of Christ. They may not reflect the character that God requires of them. According to their place in God's kingdom, they may not have the right motivation (their reason for doing what they are doing for the kingdom of God). They may be honoring God's distinct, personal will for their lives but only doing so for money, the praises of others, or self-gratification (self-pleasure, satisfaction). There are many reasons that we may be in the correct place but not properly positioned. Can you name some other reasons why we may not be positioned appropriately?

When evaluating (form an idea about) each other, people of this world mostly focus on the outward appearance, what they can see with their eyes or hear with their ears. Usually, our peers focus on our outward appearance. God is different. He only looks at our hearts, how we feel and think about things (ref. 1st Samuel 16:7). Do we truly love God and all humanity? Do we have compassion and sympathy for all others who may be suffering or hurting? Are our hearts fixed on serving, knowing, and loving Him more than all others? God knows all the feelings of our hearts and the reasons that we do what we do.

God gives us the chance to serve Him by completing His will for our lives. When we are first informed about God's distinct, personal will for our lives, it is our choice to accept His will or reject His will. God will not force His will upon us. When we accept His will, we are committing ourselves to serve Him and honor Him without reservation (holding back). This means that we are "all in" and "sold out" to God's will for our lives. With this mindset, there is no turning back. This is a life-long commitment or until God revises it. This also means that we must obey Him at all costs. These are Jesus' requirements for Christian discipleship. Accepting God's will and not obeying Him in all matters of life may result in God replacing us as He did with King Saul.

When Saul was replaced, he was saddened and grieved for the remainder of his life. There is no greater sadness than being replaced by someone else God has chosen because of our disobedience. God will complete the big pictures of His kingdom on earth with or without us as a piece of His puzzle. There is no greater honor than to be included in His desired pictures of His kingdom on earth. All of His pictures are special and are purposed to glorify Him, never ourselves. The choice to accept or reject God's requirement of obedience is ours to make. But to be included in His pictures of His kingdom on earth, we must be obedient to God, our parents, and our guardians.

****

The Bible gives us God's corporate will for our lives. However, the Bible does not give us God's distinct, personal will for our lives. Some may be wondering how they can find out what God's distinct, personal will is for their lives.

In response to this concern, we will review how each of the servants in our examples was told of God's will.

****

In our first example of Noah, God spoke to Noah and told him to build the ark (Genesis 6:14-16).

In the second example of Moses, God spoke to Moses from a burning bush and informed him of His distinct, personal will (Exodus 3:10).

In the third example of Saul and David, God sent the prophet Samuel to inform both Saul and David of His distinct, personal will and anoint them as king (1st Samuel 10:1, 16:13).

In the final example of Mary, God sent His angel Gabriel to tell her of His distinct, personal will for her to become the mother of Jesus (Luke 1:26).

(We encourage you to read each of their stories.)

In reviewing these examples from the Bible, we can see that God will use different ways and sources to inform someone of His distinct, personal will for their life. In these examples, He used one of His angels, one of His prophets, and even God himself revealed His will through a burning bush. From these examples, we can see that God will use whomsoever He chooses, and whatever way is needed to reveal His distinct, personal will. As obedient and faithful servants of God, we can be confident that He will reveal to us His distinct, personal will for our lives in some way of His choosing. In the case of this author, God spoke His distinct, personal will into his heart. God then sent other people to inform and reassure him of His will. After searching the Bible, this was found to be Biblically supported. God made us, so He knows the best way to communicate with us.

The Bible does not tell us when Jesus was told or how He found out God's distinct, personal will for Him to die on the cross for our salvation. However, we know that Jesus was informed, and this was His life's mission. Just like Jesus, God's distinct, personal will for our lives may, at times, be too difficult for us to complete with our own strength. Also, just like Jesus, God will give us the strength that is needed and as it is needed.

[82]

Just like Jesus and each of the examples that we used from the Bible, we too can and must receive God's distinct, personal will for our lives. We don't know how God will inform us or when He will inform us. But we know that he desires to tell us. We are to wait in faith as God decides the right time to let us know. It is our responsibility to ask Him if we truly want to know. As we wait, we must obey His instructions from the Bible and honor Him in all that we do. We must also obey and honor our parents and guardians. With some of us, God may not inform us until later in our life. However, we should never give up hope of knowing and never get tired of waiting on God. In God's timing, He will let us know.

Prayer:

Dear God, thank You for choosing me to be a part of the perfect pictures of Your kingdom on earth. I pray that You will help me to live out Your corporate will that is for each person in Your kingdom. I also pray that You will reveal to me Your distinct, personal will for the rest of my life on earth as You did for Your Son Jesus and His disciples. When I receive it, I ask for You to help me be obedient to all that You want me to do. I really want to be just like Jesus. Like Jesus, I know that You love me. Now allow me to demonstrate my love for You through honoring Your will for my life. This I ask for Your glory. Amen.

Questions:

1. Can you explain what it means to glorify God?
2. What is the meaning of "evangelism?"
3. From how you live your life, would your friends be surprised to know that you want to be just like Jesus? How would you feel about them knowing?
4. What is meant by the statement, "Seek first the kingdom of God and His righteousness?" Why is this important for children and youth?
5. Why was the boy Jesus surprised that His parents could not find Him?
6. Explain God's corporate will and His distinct, personal will.
7. How does God inform us of His distinct, personal will?
8. Why was King Saul replaced as king of Israel? Do you think that was fair? Why?
9. Why is it important to be correctly placed and properly positioned in the kingdom of God?
10. When God sees us, does He look at our outward appearance or our hearts? Explain.
11. What is the meaning of "holy?" Explain.
12. Why must we not worship or pray to Mary, the mother of Jesus?

Chapter 6

Honoring and Obeying Our Parents

"Then he returned to Nazareth with them and was obedient to them." Luke 2:51

At the age of twelve, Jesus provided all children and youth an example of living to please our heavenly Father. As a child, Jesus knew the corporate will of His heavenly Father and what pleased Him. Jesus knew that His heavenly Father's will was for Him to honor and obey His parents.

Our Bible talks a lot about obedience. Everyone who accepts Jesus as their Lord and Savior by committing their life to Him must be obedient to God's commandments in the Bible. This is another reason we must study the Bible, so we will know what God wants us to do and what He does not want us to do.

Many children and youth own their own Bible. If you do not own a Bible, tell your parent(s) or guardian(s) that you want to know more about God's kingdom and more about Jesus, so you would like to have your own Bible. Everyone should own their own Bible. If you are a member of a church or any other group of people who worship together, ask your pastor, group leader, or worship leader what Bible they would recommend for you to get based on your age. Usually, if they know that you do not own one, they will help you get one. It is best to get a Bible written for children or youth to make it easier for you to understand what it says and means. When you receive your own Bible, you should thank God for it, protect it, and care for it. Remember, your Bible is one way that God will speak to you as you study it. As we have already said, after you receive your own Bible, start reading it as often as you can. We recommend that you start by reading the books of John and Proverbs. Set time aside every day when you can be alone to read it and learn from it. Always pray to God to give you understanding before you start to read. If there are things in the Bible that you do not understand, be just like Jesus and ask questions to those who can help you understand. Always have someone that you can trust to give you good answers and help you to understand.

Whoever you trust to do this, be sure that your parent(s) or guardian(s) also know and trust them. Talk to your parent(s) or guardian(s) first before searching for someone to help you understand. Always seek your parent's or guardian's permission, guidance, and understanding in all matters of life. Remember, God has given them the responsibility to raise you and help you become a responsible adult, one who knows Him and serves Him. God tells our parents, ***"Teach a child to choose the right path, and when he is older he will remain upon it"*** (Proverbs 22:6). If our parent(s) love and honor God, they will be obedient to what God instructs them to do. We honor God when we honor

[86]

and obey the responsibilities (commandments) that He gives us.

As servants of God, He requires all of us to be obedient to Him. His instructions that we must follow are in the Bible. Also, as earlier stated, accepting God's distinct, personal will for our lives requires our obedience. The Bible talks a lot about obedience. In this writing, we have talked a lot about obedience. In chapter one, we gave a simple definition of "obey."

So what is "obedience?"

****

"Obedience" is responding to someone's authority over you or honoring (respecting) someone's responsibility for you, or acknowledging someone's position or status in life by doing what they tell you to do. Obedience is the ultimate honor that you can give someone and the primary way to show your love for God. Obedience is following their orders, commands, laws, or requests (a request implies that they may ask politely).

****

The Bible talks a lot about God's requirement for obedience and the need to follow His commandments. When we do not follow God's commandments, we are **rebelling** (willfully resisting) against God's authority. It angers God when we live in rebellion against His authority, as was shown in the example of King Saul in the previous chapter. When we live a lifestyle of worldliness by entertaining the things of this world, we live in rebellion against God (James 4:4, 1st John 2:15).

[87]

When we think of how loving God is and how good and faithful He is to us, we should want to please Him by avoiding all forms of worldliness and obeying His commandments. We should experience joy and satisfaction (fulfillment, pleasure) when we obey him.

Also, as children and youth who love God, God wants us to be obedient to everyone He has given His authority and placed over our lives, especially our parents and guardians. As earlier stated, when we obey them, we honor God. God commands all children and youth to obey their parents.

In Colossians 3:20, God tells all children and youth, *"You children must always obey your fathers and mothers, for that pleases the Lord."* In Ephesians 6:1-3, God tells all children and youth, *"Children obey your parents; this is the right thing to do because God has placed them in authority over you. Honor your father and mother. This is the first of God's Ten Commandments that ends with a promise. And this is the promise: that if you honor your father and mother, yours will be a long life, full of blessing."*

As we review these commandments of God, two things should be noted. First, God is pleased when children and youth obey their parents. Second, when children and youth honor their parents, God promises them a long life on this earth and many blessings. God will always honor His promises when the conditions that He requires are met. Rebellion against God will lead to a lack of His oversight and protection in our lives and often unnecessary confusion and sadness.

When we observe the troubling signs of our times, we can see a Biblical reason and a disturbing parallel for many of the regretful problems that children and youth are currently experiencing. The rate of homicides, suicides, and willful drug overdoses among children and youth in America is at an all-time high.

Homicide is when one human being deliberately causes the death of another (e.g., murder).

Suicide is death caused by injuring oneself with the intent to die (taking one's own life).

A **drug overdose** is taking too much of a substance, whether prescription, over-the-counter, legal, or illegal (willful drug overdoses among children and youth primarily are attempts to end their life).

Researchers from the U.S. Centers for Disease Control and Prevention revealed that the death rate for suicides of those ages 10 to 24 rose 56 percent between 2007 and 2017. The rate of homicides for this same age group increased by 18 percent from 2015 to 2017. The CDC also reported that teen drug overdose deaths rose 19 percent from 2014 to 2015 in the United States.

The Population Reference Bureau (PRB) reported, "While drug overdoses and drug-related deaths are much more common among adults than children, it is likely that millions of children have been affected by the epidemic, either directly – through parental addiction or death – or indirectly through the experiences of friends, classmates, or neighbors."

These untimely deaths are not just public health concerns but also symptoms of spiritual crises that exist among America's children and youth. Usually, worldly solutions (medication or psychiatric intervention) are considered when symptoms of concern are detected. However, these troubling concerns are spiritual problems requiring spiritual solutions for life-long oneness with Christ and spiritual well-being.

All three of these regretful and sad realities that exist among today's children and youth are due to spiritual confusion. **Spiritual confusion** is unawareness of who God really is and uncertainty or a lack of understanding of one's status or potential with God.

Many of these untimely deaths are often due to a lack of Godly love in their lives that can result in feelings of anger, depression, and/or hopelessness. These feelings can often be traced back to dysfunction (not normal relationships according to Biblical principles) within relationships and the family unit. In this present cultural climate of open rebellion in our society, many of America's children and youth do not honor authority, including the authority of their parents. As a result, many live outside of the covenant promise of protection from God (Ephesians 6:3). Without God's oversight and protection, they are helplessly exposed to the convincing evil strategies of confusion orchestrated by Satan. Because of the resulting frustrations (feeling of hopelessness caused by the inability to do or receive something they desire outside of God's will) from his strategies, the inward feeling of not caring for others and/or themselves becomes evident in their lives. This often regretful outcome of emotional confusion reflects the success of the enemy's age-old strategies that often lead to regretful decisions and, all too often, self-destruction. This is just one of several possibilities.

As we know from the word of God, all homicides, suicides, and willful drug overdoses result from Satan's evil influence and reflect the success of his strategies and intentions. The word of God reminds us that Satan's purpose is to kill, steal and destroy. It also reminds us that Jesus' purpose is to give life in all its fullness (John 10:10). Children and youth can never receive the fullness of life that Jesus desires for them and its benefits (including God's oversight and His protection from evil) while living in rebellion against the commandments of God. The lives of many of our children and youth are ending too soon because they do not honor God's authority and accept His commandments as a way of life. Many do not truly love their parent(s) and guardian(s), which is revealed in them not honoring their God-given authority.

There are Biblical truths that all children and youth need to know, understand, and remember.

Every human life is sacred and precious to our loving Father. God is the giver and sustainer of all life. God desires that children and youth live their lives to their fullness, according to His will, and under His care. Children and youth must realize that they do not have God's authority to destroy human life, even their own. To do so is sin. Though others may not understand, children and youth need to realize that God understands their concerns, and they can trust Him in all situations. More than anyone else, He knows what they are going through. There is nothing in this world that they cannot overcome with His help. God can make all things new.

All children and youth need to know that though they may not receive the love or understanding they desire from others, including their parents or guardians, God loves them unconditionally, and there is nothing they can do to separate themselves from His love.

These are Biblical truths of the word of God and truths on which all children and youth can stand and live with hope for their future.

As a reminder, Ephesians 6:3 is God's assuring commandment for children and youth that comes with His promise and commitment to them for long life on this earth and His blessings.

Also, God tells us in Proverbs 1:8, *"Listen, my son, to your father's instruction and do not forsake your mother's teaching"* (NIV). Again, God tells all children and youth in Proverbs 23:22, *"Listen to your father, who gave you life, and do not despise your mother when she is old"* (NIV).

When children and youth obey these commandments of God, His oversight and favor will be experienced in all areas of their lives. These are God's commandments for children and youth (and adults with living parents) that He has provided in the Bible.

When we read God's commandments for all children and youth, there are two things that we can see that are very important to God regarding their relationship with their parents. God commands all children and youth to **obey** their parents and **honor** their parents. Even after we are adults, God requires that we honor our parents (ref. Proverbs 23:22). Giving honor to our parents is a life-long requirement of God

[92]

and again, was given with His promise of long life and blessings.

We obey our parents (and guardians) when we do what they tell or want (imply) us to do **(The assumption is that our parents are God-fearing and will only tell us to do what God approves)**. We disobey our parents when we do not do what they tell or want (imply) us to do. When we disobey our parents, we are rebelling against God because we are going against God's commandments. God still loves us, but He hates all sin.

****

What does it mean to honor our parents? To **honor our parents** is to admire them, to treat them with respect, and to show our appreciation to them. It is having a high regard for our parents and recognizing their God-given authority and value to us and their value to God.

There are many ways that we honor our parents:

1. We honor them by obeying them.
2. We honor them by respecting them.
3. We honor them when we do things to make them proud of us.
4. We honor them by spending time with them.
5. We honor them by listening to their stories.
6. We honor them by telling them how much we love them.
7. We honor them by helping them to do things around the house.
8. We honor them by having fun with them.
9. We honor them by going with them to church.

[93]

10. We honor them by going shopping with them.
11. We honor them by running errands for them.
12. We honor them by complimenting them.
13. We honor them by lowering the volume of our music or activities while in their presence.
14. We honor them by being patient with them and taking care of their needs when they are ill or getting older.
15. We honor them by praying with them and for them.

These are just some of the ways that we honor our parents. There are many more ways we can honor them.

This was the attitude of the boy Jesus. After his parents found him in the Temple, He could have dishonored them. He could have done so by being angry with them for disrupting His time of sitting before the teachers and learning from them because this was what He enjoyed. We must avoid becoming angry with our parents. He could have dishonored them by showing pride and ranking Himself above them by reminding them Who He really was, the Son of God. He could have rebelled against their desires for Him to accompany them back to Nazareth after spending the last few days on His own and seeing after His own needs. He could have told them that He didn't need them anymore because His heavenly Father would take care of Him. There were many ways that He could have dishonored His parents. However, He chose not to dishonor them.

Luke 2:51 states, ***"Then he returned to Nazareth with them and was obedient to them."*** Rather than dishonor His parents, he honored the authority and the responsibility that His heavenly Father had given to His parents (Ephesians 6:1) and willingly returned to Nazareth with them. At this particular instance, this was the supreme way of showing honor to them. Not only did the boy Jesus honor His parents by returning with them, but He honored the will of His heavenly Father by being obedient to them.

To our heavenly Father, obedience is the most important thing that we can do to show our love for Him. When we obey God, our parents, and our guardians, God is pleased.

If we want to be just like Jesus, we must also show our love for our heavenly Father by honoring and obeying our parents and guardians and being obedient to His commandments in the Bible.

Yes, we can be just like Jesus.

Prayer: *(If your parents are deceased, you may pray this prayer for your guardians)*

Heavenly Father, I have not obeyed everything that my parents have wanted me to do. Neither have I honored them as I should. By disobeying and not honoring them, I have dishonored You by not obeying your commandments to me in the Bible. Please forgive me. I now know that I must obey and honor my parents because of the authority and responsibility that You have given them over me and because of Your commandments. I realize that this is how I show my love and respect for You and them. I also realize how blessed I am and how special they are. I thank You for my parents and ask for Your guidance, favor, and protection over their lives. From this day on, with Your help and oversight, I will always obey them and honor them. Amen.

****

Questions:

1. What are the two things that God commands all children and youth to do regarding their parents?
2. Can you explain what they mean?
3. What does it mean to rebel against God? How does God respond to rebellion?
4. What is the meaning of spiritual confusion?
5. What are homicides? Suicides? What is the meaning of drug overdose?
6. Why do you think the rates for homicides, suicides, and drug overdoses are so high among children and youth in America? What can you suggest as a solution to this problem?
7. Can you think of a time when you disobeyed your parents? How did you feel?
8. We have listed ways that you can honor your parents. Can you think of some other ways?
9. Can you think of things that will dishonor your parents? Can you think of anything in your past that has dishonored your parents? If yes, what should you do?

Chapter 7

Receiving and Growing in Wisdom

"So Jesus grew both tall and wise, and was loved by God and man." Luke 2:52

As a child, Jesus grew in wisdom and was blessed by God and humanity.

In chapter two, we briefly talked about wisdom. We said that wisdom is the ability to make good decisions. It is good sound judgment and knowing the right things to do.

Contrary to popular belief that there are three types of wisdom, there are only two major types. There is Godly wisdom, and there is worldly wisdom. Godly wisdom deals with advancing the things of God and the kingdom of God. Worldly wisdom deals with advancing the evil ways of this world. In this writing, we are only discussing Godly wisdom.

God said in Proverbs 3:21-26, *"Have two goals: wisdom – that is, knowing and doing right – and common sense. Don't let them slip away, for they fill you with living energy, and are a feather in your cap. They keep you safe from defeat and disaster and from stumbling off the trail. With them on guard you can sleep without fear; you need not be afraid of disaster or the plots of wicked men, for the Lord is with you; he protects you."*

God is instructing us to get wisdom, and He is telling us why we need it and the promise of His presence and protection to those who have it. Since God primarily speaks to us through the Bible, we need the Bible to tell us how to gain wisdom.

Proverbs 1:7-9 states, *"How does a man become wise? The first step is to trust and reverence the Lord! Only fools refuse to be taught. Listen to your father and mother. What you learn from them will stand you in good stead; it will gain you many honors."*

God tells us that the first step to becoming wise is to trust Him. Proverbs 3:4-5 states, *"If you want favor with both God and man, and a reputation for good judgment and common sense, then trust the Lord completely; don't ever trust yourself."* Luke 2:52 informs us that the boy Jesus was blessed with the favor (KJV) of God and man. This implies that Jesus trusted God completely. So, if we want to be just like Jesus, we must also learn to trust God completely.

But what does it mean to **trust God**? As earlier stated, to trust God means to believe everything that He says. You must believe that everything the Bible says about God is true. You must believe God can do everything that the Bible says that He can do. You must believe God will do everything that the Bible says He will do. When God tells us to trust Him completely, it means that we must not have any doubt about God, what He says, and what He promises. We must be like Shadrach, Meshach, and Abednego in chapter one. As we grow in life, we learn to trust God more each day. We grow to trust Him more and more as we see and understand what God is doing each day all around us, what He has done and continues to do. Each day, we should observe and note the faithfulness of God.

When we see the sunrise each morning and set each evening, we see more and more how reliable (capable of being trusted or depended on) God is. God holds the earth in place as it rotates around the sun. God keeps the earth from getting too close to the hot sun or falling away from the warmth of the sun. If the earth gets too close to the sun, everything, including us, will burn up. If the earth falls too far from the warmth of the sun, everything, including us, will freeze. God keeps the earth at the perfect distance from the sun, and He has faithfully done this since He created this world. When we see leaves fall from the trees every fall and we see the trees grow new leaves every spring, once again, we see God's reliability. Again, He has faithfully done this since the creation.

Only God can do what is impossible for humans to do. There is nothing in this world that is too difficult for God to understand, handle, or change. Each day and each year of our lives, we see how reliable God is and the great things He does, so we believe that He will continue doing what He has always done. We should develop more trust in Him each passing day of our lives. When we see that God always does what He

[99]

says, we develop more trust in Him. It becomes easier to trust Him completely when we look at how reliable He is and has always been. Can you think of other things that God does?

****

When God says, *"Don't ever trust yourself,"* He means you are never to trust what you think or reason, but only trust what the Bible says because the Bible only says what God says. Everything that God says is true. If what you think or believe agrees with the Bible, only then can you trust yourself.

We can't trust ourselves because much of our thinking and reasoning is affected by the influence of worldliness. We think and reason according to what we are primarily exposed to in life. For most of the children and youth in America who consider themselves Christian, their exposure to the Bible and the teachings of God is mainly on Sunday mornings. The remainder of their time is mostly characterized by worldliness (partaking of and enjoying the things and ways of this world). Understandably, their thinking and reasoning in life cannot be viewed as having the influence of God but the influence of this world.

The Bible reminds us that those who are friends with this world are God's enemies. James 4:4 states, *"You adulterous people, don't you know that friendship with the world is hatred toward God? Anyone who chooses to be a friend of the world becomes an enemy of God"* (NIV). John states in 1st John 2:15-17, *"Stop loving this evil world and all that*

[100]

it offers you, for when you love these things you show that you do not really love God; for all these worldly things, these evil desires – the craze for sex, the ambition to buy everything that appeals to you, and the pride that comes from wealth and importance – these are not from God. They are from this evil world itself. And this world is fading away, and these evil, forbidden things will go with it, but whoever keeps doing the will of God will live forever."

****

As a word of caution, all children and youth who desire to be a disciple of Jesus must avoid all forms of worldliness. You cannot partake of the evil pleasures, the things, and ways of this world and be a disciple of Jesus. Jesus requires a total allegiance (loyalty, commitment) to Him and God's kingdom.

****

There are a total of one hundred and sixty-eight hours in each week. If children and youth are only exposed to Biblical teaching for one and a half hours on Sunday mornings, this represents less than one percent of their total time. The influence of less than one percent is so small that it can't be considered a significant factor. Their actual time spent in the word of God must be considered as non-existing. (A more depressing truth about this matter is that, in the average church, the one and a half hours that children and youth spend in church on Sunday mornings are not really spent in Biblical study.) Therefore, it is naive of

[101]

anyone to believe that Biblical principles will guide their actions in life.

Add to this depressing reality the influence of ungodly peer pressure. It then becomes easier to understand the ungodliness of children and youth seen in the daily news headlines, even among those who profess to know God. Indeed, much prayer is required for children and youth in America. Still, prayer must be supplemented by a total refocus on the importance of cross-centered, Biblical education and actual time spent with God.

There is an expression in the dietary field that says, "we are what we eat." In applying this understanding to Christian discipleship, "we are what we learn." Our learning is generally paralleled to where most of our time is spent. If ninety-nine percent of our time is spent in a lifestyle and environment of worldliness, then our thinking and reasoning will be worldly.

The Bible gives a crucial requirement of Jesus for Christian discipleship in John 15, verses 4 & 8. Jesus states, *"Take care to live in me, and let me live in you. For a branch can't produce fruit when severed from the vine. Nor can you be fruitful apart from me. My true disciples produce bountiful harvests. This brings great glory to my Father."*

In this requirement for discipleship and bearing fruit (good results from our labor) for God's kingdom, Jesus commands us to live (remain) in Him and allow Him to live in us.

When we entertain a lifestyle of worldliness, we do not remain in Him, and we do not allow Jesus to live in us. When we live a lifestyle of worldliness, we become severed (detached, cut) from Jesus, our vine of spiritual nourishment and guidance, and we then become worldly. In a state of worldliness, we can never trust ourselves. True Godly wisdom will only be realized when we detach ourselves from all worldliness and commit ourselves totally to God and trust Him only.

****

The next requirement that God gives for becoming wise is to have reverence for Him. To have **reverence for God** means that we have great love, honor, and respect for Him. It means that we think very highly of God, more highly than anyone else. It means that God has the primary place in our hearts, and all that we do in life is for His glory. Our reverence for God must be greater than our reverence for anyone or anything else.

We show our reverence for God by how we treat Him in our day-to-day lives. When we casually use God's name in our conversations, we are then irreverent. When we use God's name in curse words, we are again irreverent. **Irreverence** is being disrespectful, not giving due respect to God. God is offended by all acts of disrespect for Him.

All children and youth who desire Christian discipleship and God's wisdom must be very careful in their everyday activities not to disrespect God. We show reverence for God by taking His hatred for sin and all ungodliness seriously. We show our reverence for God by learning to worship Him with a truthful and honest heart and a sacrificial love for each other and all of His creation. We show our reverence for God by loving Him with all of our heart, soul, mind, and strength.

When we willfully come to church late or leave early, we are showing irreverence for God. Willful tardiness (coming late) and impatience (unwillingness to remain) show a lack of reverence and love for God. Those who genuinely love God will cherish every moment that can be spent in public worship with other true believers. Rather than come late, they will arrive early to pray and prepare themselves to be in God's presence. Rather than leave early, they will remain to reflect and pray about their experience in worship and fellowship with other worshippers.

Every true church of Christ and disciple of Christ will have no tolerance for disrespect for God. We show reverence for God by desiring to spend as much time as is possible with Him, whether in public worship or private worship. God designed us as creatures of worship. God requires that we worship Him only. When we cease to worship God, we then begin to worship other things. Our lives are spent in unceasing worship. Worship to God should be our greatest joy. God honors our worship to Him.

In today's version of Christianity, reverence for God is not prioritized to the level of seriousness that the

Bible requires. Without the Biblically required reverence for God, we will not receive His wisdom.

****

Once we have complete trust in God and reverence for Him, then God tells us, *"**Listen to your father and mother. What you learn from them will stand you in good stead; it will gain you many honors"*** (Proverbs 1:8-9).

When we learn to listen to our fathers and mothers, we learn to respect authority. God has given our parents not only the responsibility of raising us, but He has also given them His authority (the right to give orders, make decisions, or take action when needed). So when we listen to our parents, we are learning to respect their authority and all authority. As we grow in life, we must learn to respect and yield to authority.

Many children and youth get in legal trouble because they have not learned to respect and yield to authority. Law enforcement has the authority to maintain law and order. They have the authority to use whatever legal means is necessary to do so. So, it is important for all children and youth to learn to honor and respect authority which begins with listening to their parents and guardians.

Listening to our parents and guardians implies that we will trust their wisdom and knowledge and abide (accept and act in agreement with) by their rules and obey them in all concerns of life. When we learn to abide by their rules, we learn the importance of rules and the importance of following all rules in life.

Rules are required to maintain order and stability (firm and steady, not likely to give way or come apart) in our homes, in the world, and in the kingdom of God. Even as an adult, we will have rules and regulations that we must follow. Also, as an adult, we will be subject to authority, whether it is the authority of God, the authority of the law, the authority of our supervisors at our employment, or the authority of anyone to whom we are subject to in life. All authority in life is under God's authority. The ability to accept and function under authority begins with listening to our parents.

God also said, *"**What you learn from them will stand you in good stead; it will gain you many honors**"* (Proverbs 1:9). Here, God gives you the good results from listening to your parents. **Listening to our parents implies obeying them.** God is basically saying that when you learn to listen to your parents, the things that you learn from them will place you in a good position in life. The things that you learn from them will give you much favor among humanity and provide many honors in your life. Their wisdom and knowledge will open many doors of opportunity for you in life.

****

God said that the first step for getting wisdom is trusting Him entirely and having reverence for Him. Then God said that we must listen to our parents.

[106]

Finally, God said in Proverbs 2:1, *"Every young man who listens to me and obeys my instructions will be given wisdom and good sense."* In this scripture, God gave us His last two requirements for receiving wisdom. We must also listen to Him for instructions, and we must obey His instructions.

As we have said before, the best way to listen to God is by studying the Bible. God mainly speaks to us as we study the Bible.

****

After listening to God, He then requires us to obey Him. As we said in chapter one, **obey** means to carry out the commands, orders, instructions, or wishes of someone else. In other words, we must do what God tells us to do.

When we fulfill these five requirements of God, He will give us wisdom just as He did with the boy Jesus. After receiving wisdom from God, we are required to increase our wisdom or to grow in wisdom.

We **grow in wisdom** from the things we experience in life, from studying the Bible, and, just like Jesus, from listening to and learning from others who have wisdom.

Many of the problems that we have as children and youth happen because of a lack of wisdom. Also, many of the problems that we experience as children and youth happen because of peer pressure.

A **"peer"** is someone close to your age, an equal, usually a friend or an associate. **"Peer pressure"** is being influenced by someone from your peer group, usually a friend, to change your values, attitude, or behavior to agree with theirs because you want to be accepted by them. Peer pressure is the number one reason for bad decisions among children and youth. Children and youth have been found to mostly make bad decisions when they feel pressured by or seek the acceptance or attention of their friends. To most children and youth, to be accepted by their friends is more desired than to be accepted by God.

As children and youth who want to be just like Jesus, we can never allow our friends to change our God-focused values, attitude, or behavior. We must always keep God as the focus for all of our decisions and actions in life. We should never allow our friends to influence us to do anything that would not be pleasing to God. It must remain our desire to please God above all others, especially our friends. As their true friend, rather than yielding to their negative influence, we should use every opportunity to introduce and direct them to God.

When we grow in wisdom, God will bless us as He blessed the boy Jesus. When others see God's blessings in our lives and His favor over all that we do, they will be drawn to us and want to know more about the God we serve. When they see how much we trust God and reverence Him, they too will begin to trust God and reverence Him because they will want what they see in us.

Once they discover and understand God, they will love us, bless us and honor us as the one who led them out of the darkness and evilness of this world to the wonderful light of God, just like people did with the boy Jesus.

Prayer:

Father God, I now understand why I need wisdom. I do desire to be able to make the right choices and decisions in my life. I ask for Your help in completing Your five requirements for Godly wisdom. There have been times that I have not made good decisions in my life. Please forgive me. I understand that I must be careful about peer pressure and how it can lead to me making bad decisions in life. Help me not yield to peer pressure but to show my peers the right way in life by leading them to You. Use me as a vessel of change for all of my peers that need to know You. I do want to please You in all that I do. Thank You for all that You do for me. Amen.

Questions:

1. What are the two types of wisdom? Explain.
2. Why do we need wisdom? What is God's promise to those who have wisdom?
3. In this chapter we listed some of the things that God does for us. Can you think of other things that He does for you?
4. What does it mean to trust God?
5. What did God mean when He said, "Don't ever trust yourself?"
6. Can you explain why worldliness is harmful to Christian discipleship?
7. What does it mean to have reverence for God? Irreverence for God? Can you give examples?
8. Why do we need rules?
9. What is the meaning of peer pressure?
10. What are God's five requirements for receiving wisdom? Can you explain what they mean?
11. How do we grow in wisdom?

———————————————————————

Chapter 8

Summary

"Yes, I Can Be Just Like Jesus"

"for I can do everything God asks me to with the help of Christ who gives me the strength and power." Philippians 4:13

When we choose to become just like Jesus, we begin the process of Christian discipleship. We must begin to see Jesus as not just our Savior, Lord, and best friend but as our new model for how we will live our lives here on earth. We are choosing to turn from the evil things of this world and commit our lives entirely to God so that Jesus can live through us.

Christian disciples must view themselves as soldiers and warriors preparing for warfare. We must accept the reality that we live in a world that is hostile toward Jesus and those who believe in Him. Jesus has warned us that as His disciples, we will be persecuted. **Persecute** means to treat cruelly or harshly for holding certain beliefs or ideas (for believing in Jesus).

Jesus warned His disciples about persecution when He said to them in John 15:17-21, *"I demand that you love each other, for you get enough hate from the world! But then, it hated me before it hated you. The world would love you if you belonged to it; but you don't – for I chose you to come out of the world, and so it hates you. Do you remember what I told you? A slave isn't greater than his master! So since they persecuted me, naturally they will persecute you. And if they had listened to me, they would listen to you! The people of the world will persecute you because you belong to me, for they don't know God who sent me."*

When we are persecuted as disciples of Christ, we must remember that it is not us that people hate. It is Jesus living through us that they hate. As has been since the days of Christ, this world remains hostile toward Him and those who believe in Him. This evil world crucified Jesus on a cross because of His righteousness. All twelve of the first-century disciples of Jesus were persecuted because of their commitment to Him and God's kingdom on earth.

Christian disciples are in a war in America and around the world. America is a spiritual war zone. The battle is between righteousness and evil. When we read the local and worldwide news, evil seems to be winning. However, with children and youth serving in the renewed army of Christ, this will not continue.

Children and youth are dying at record numbers each day because of spiritual warfare. **Spiritual warfare** is fighting against Satan and His evil forces. We do not fight physically because our enemies are not flesh and blood (human). Though mainly operating through humans and unseen, they do exist (ref.

Ephesians 6:12) (e.g., anyone lying, sowing division, or hatred). Spiritual warfare is the ongoing battle between righteousness and evil for control over people's lives. Continuous and effective prayer to our heavenly Father is an essential weapon for Jesus' disciples during the ongoing struggles of spiritual warfare (Ephesians 6:18). Therefore, we must always pray for renewal, God's protection, wisdom, and directions.

Children and youth of this world must be fully prepared and equipped for battle. Generally, churches enable Satan by not purposefully directing their children's and youth's focus to the sacrificial cross of Christ and its power. As for all believers, the power of the cross is available to them for victorious warfare living. Instead, many churches mainly direct their focus to a never-ending cycle of less challenging and less important matters of the faith, things that are considered to be more entertaining. In some instances, they direct them away from the faith through the use of worldly animated (cartoon), Disney, and superhero characters. As a result, the children and youth are literally losing the many spiritual battles of life simply because of a lack of spiritual awareness.

There is a song that many of us adults learned in church when we were children. The title of the song is "We Are Soldiers." The lyrics are:

"We are soldiers in the army. We have to fight, although we have to cry. We've got to hold up the blood-stained banner. We've got to hold it up until we die!"

[113]

We enjoyed singing that song in church as children even though we did not truly understand its meaning. However, the depressing headlines of today's news from around the world bring its true meaning and relevance into clear focus. In teaching children this song, we must wonder if religious leaders of earlier years had better spiritual clarity regarding children and youth's Biblical role and needs. This song highlights the required mission for Christian discipleship in the twenty-first century, especially for children and youth. **The required mission is to create new soldiers for the army of Christ who are committed to holding up His blood-stained banner, his selfless, sacrificial life.**

Indeed, Christian discipleship must be viewed as warfare ministry because we face a real enemy in Satan who only comes to kill, steal and destroy. Jesus informed His disciples of this fact in John 10:10. As a reminder, He said, ***"The thief's purpose is to steal, kill and destroy. My purpose is to give life in all its fullness."*** This statement of Jesus clearly identified the two opposing forces in this war and revealed their goals. Still today, our enemies, as believers in Christ, are Satan and his army of demons. Satan clearly is not able to fight Jesus one-on-one. So His only strategy is to attack those who believe in Jesus. He attacks children and youth because they represent the hopeful future of the church of God in Christ and this world.

His strategies are to tempt us to commit sin or deceive us into believing something that is not true about God and His kingdom through misinformation. Both strategies, when successful, can yield disastrous results in the lives of God's children and youth. The daily news headlines serve as evidence of this fact. As revealed in chapter six, our children and youth are committing suicide and killing each other at an alarming rate. The confusion orchestrated (masterminded) by Satan is evident in their lives. Therefore, we must continually pray to God, our source for renewed strength, understanding, protection, and required provisions for waging victorious spiritual warfare. Also, we must commit ourselves to God through continuous study of the Bible to know the truth regarding God and His kingdom and understanding our weapons of warfare (ref. Ephesians 6:10-18).

Satan knows that God hates sin. He also knows that he can affect our lives and our relationship with God if he can convince us to sin continually. His goal is to destroy our relationship with God and our eternal salvation in Heaven. We must always be on guard for his attacks. Peter issued a warning to all disciples of Christ. He wrote in 1st Peter 5:8, *"Be careful – watch out for attacks from Satan, your great enemy. He prowls around like a hungry, roaring lion, looking for some victim to tear apart. Stand firm when he attacks. Trust the Lord; and remember that other Christians all around the world are going through these sufferings too."* In this warning, Peter said, "when" he attacks, not "if" he attacks. He warns that we will be attacked if we are Christians.

As disciples of Christ, especially children and youth, we must be forever mindful that Satan is not a

[115]

symbol for evil but an actual living being whose only intent is death, theft, and destruction.

****

Even though we are not adults, we must realize, as did the boy Jesus, God has assigned to each of us something special that He wants us to do to advance His kingdom on earth in the midst of growing opposition. We are all very important to God. However, we must remain **humble**, never feeling that we are more important than anyone else. God gives special blessings to the humble. We are all children and youth of God and precious in His sight. Our lives have a purpose, and God has a unique plan for each of us in His end-time army for His kingdom on earth.

To prepare ourselves to receive God's plan for our lives, we must be obedient and grow in knowledge, wisdom, and faith. We must learn all that we can about God's kingdom by following the example of the boy Jesus. Just like the boy Jesus we prepare ourselves by;

1. **Taking care of our responsibilities.**
2. **Learning from our mistakes.**
3. **Learning to listen, and asking questions when we do not understand.**
4. **Studying to gain understanding so that we can give good answers to our teachers' questions and our world's problems.**
5. **Knowing that our heavenly Father's business is the most important thing in our lives.**
6. **Honoring and obeying our parents or guardians.**

[116]

7. Receiving and growing in Godly wisdom.

These are the seven keys the boy Jesus gave to all children and youth desiring to be 'just like Him.'

****

Christian discipleship is not easy. It requires much sacrifice. It requires learning to see this world and the things of this world as Jesus sees them. It requires responding to the needs of this world as Jesus did and still does. It requires loving our heavenly Father more than anything else in this world, as Jesus does. It requires loving all others more than we love ourselves, as Jesus does. It requires giving up the things of this world that many of us had come to enjoy in our past life. In our past life, we lived for this world and the things of this world before committing our lives to Christ.

****

The most difficult part of Christian discipleship is turning completely from all worldliness and totally committing our lives to Christ. From the beginning of our time on earth, we are taught by the world to live for ourselves and the things of this world. We are taught that the things and the pleasures of this world are to be desired.

What does the world teach us?

- It teaches us to live for ourselves and to get as many worldly things as we can get in life.
- It teaches us that the more worldly things we have or experience in life, the more joy we have.
- It teaches us to value and seek worldly wisdom.

[117]

- It teaches us to accumulate and value the things of this world more than the things of God.
- It teaches us to find our security (feeling of being safe, free from danger) in the things of this world and the ways of this world.
- It teaches us the more money we have, the more secure we are in life.
- It teaches us to love ourselves above all others.
- It teaches us that the best things in this world can be bought with money; therefore, we must get as much money as possible.
- It teaches us that our biological family is more important and to be loved more than God.
- It teaches us to trust in humanity.
- It teaches us to be self-sufficient (needing no outside help).
- It teaches us that only the strong will survive.
- It teaches us to seek fame and fortune and the praises of humanity at any cost.

These are just some of the things that the world teaches us every day. Many of us must admit that we have been trained very well and lured into a life-focus and lifestyle of worldliness.

How does the world teach us these things?

The world teaches us these things from commercials, movies, sitcoms, game shows, talent and strength competitions, and music videos as we watch television or listen to the radio. It teaches us these things as we surf the internet and on billboards as we ride in our vehicles. It teaches us these things from many of the written articles and advertisements in magazines and newspapers. It teaches us through sports, competition, and the games that we play, including video games. It teaches us through many notable awards and recognitions. Perhaps, hard to believe, it even teaches us through some ministries such as the false prosperity ministries that have grown in popularity. These ministries have done much damage to the body of Christ by disregarding the true message from the sacrificial cross of Christ. Instead, they have created a self-focused message of worldly prosperity. The cross of Christ has been cosmetically altered (beautified) and given the well-received role of accessory jewelry to enhance our excessive wardrobes. Many parents unknowingly teach their children by modeling and living examples of worldliness before them. The message that we hear and receive from many worldly sources as we live each day is, "To be happy and whole, we must desire the things of this world and live a lifestyle of worldliness."

****

The Bible teaches just the opposite for Christian discipleship and developing the character of Christ. To be just like Jesus, it teaches;

- We must **not** live for ourselves but for God and all others. Living for the needs of all others is called living sacrificially (just like Jesus).
- True joy comes from being in the presence of God, not from worldly things (ref. Psalm 16:11).
- We must forsake all that we have in this world for the needs of all others. We must be willing

[119]

to give up everything we have for those in need (ref. Luke 14:33, Matthew 19:27, 25:45).

- We must desire Godly wisdom, not the wisdom of this world.
- God is our only true security in life, not worldly security (ref. Psalm 91:9-12, Prov. 3:26).
- We must love all others more than we love ourselves (ref. John 13:34,35, Eph. 5:2). This means that we will do whatever we can to ensure that everyone in this world has what they need. This was what Jesus meant when He commanded us to love all others as He loves us to become His disciple. It means that we see ourselves as stewards and all of our possessions as belonging to God. Our possessions are to be dedicated and used for His glory according to His will as He instructs us.
- We must love our heavenly Father with all our heart, soul, mind, and strength (ref. Mark 12:28-31). Our total love for God must be shown in everything about us.
- We must commit ourselves to God above all others and all else, including our family (ref. Luke 14:26, Matthew 10:37). Indeed, we are to love our family, but never more than we love God.
- We must trust the Lord entirely and never trust ourselves (ref. Proverbs 3:5).
- All we have comes from God (ref. Rom. 11:36).
- God's strength is revealed through our weakness (ref. 2nd Corinthians 12:9).
- We must first seek God's will for our lives before making any other decisions about our

lives (ref. Matthew 6:33). God and His plan for our lives must always be our priority in life.

- Just like Jesus, we must bear our cross (ref. Luke 14:27, Matthew 10:38). Our cross is that hardship that we accept when we become a disciple of Jesus (e.g., Luke 9:57-58).
- We must remain in the word of God (ref. John 8:31). Staying in the word of God means constantly studying our Bible and learning about God and His kingdom.
- We must bear fruit for the kingdom of God (ref. John 15:8). Bearing fruit is the good result that God requires from our work in His kingdom. Our fruit is the proof of our faith.
- We must win (souls), not for the praises of humanity or fame or fortune, but the kingdom of God and His glory, and at all cost.

****

As already stated, false prosperity ministries have done much damage to the body of Christ. The Bible warns us about false ministries. Romans 16:17-18 state, *"Stay away from those who cause divisions and are upsetting people's faith, teaching things about Christ that are contrary to what you have been taught. Such teachers are not working for our Lord Jesus, but only want gain for themselves. They are good speakers, and simple-minded people are often fooled by them"* (ref. 2nd Corinthians 11:13-15). Paul warned young Timothy about false prosperity ministries. Paul stated in 1st Timothy 6:5-11, *"These arguers – their minds warped by sin – don't know how to tell the* *truth; to them the Good News is just a means of making money. <u>Keep away from them.</u> Do you want to be truly rich? You already are if you are happy and good. After all, we didn't bring any money with us when we came into the world, and we can't carry away a single penny when we die. So we should be well satisfied without money if we have enough food and clothing. But people who long to be rich soon begin to do all kinds of wrong things to get money, things that hurt them and make them evil-minded and finally send them to hell itself. For the love of money is the first step toward all kinds of sin. Some people have even turned away from God because of their love for it, and as a result have pierced themselves with many sorrows. Oh, Timothy, you are God's man. Run from all these evil things and work instead at what is right and good, learning to trust him and love others, and to be patient and gentle."* All believers must be mindful of Paul's warnings and stay away from all false ministries and teachings that ignore or distort the true meaning of the sacrificial cross of Christ and its impact on their lives. These ministries are deceptions of the enemy and are not a part of God's kingdom. All who desire Christian discipleship must avoid them.

The Bible teaches us that life's real purpose and value is not from getting more things and worldly pleasures out of life but from sacrificially serving the Lord by providing for the needs of all others (ref. Matthew 20:25-28, 25:31-46). After all, that is what Jesus came to do and showed us how to do.

As disciples of Christ, we must begin to see ourselves as Christian stewards whom Jesus has chosen to manage His affairs and resources until He returns (Matthew 25:14-30, Luke 19:11-27). We must manage them knowing that we will stand before God one day and explain everything we have done and everything we have failed to do [(e.g., taking care of those in need) (ref. Matthew 25:31-46)]. We must manage them with the understanding that we will either be rewarded or punished for our stewardship (Revelation 20:12-15).

Christian discipleship requires doing everything within our power always to honor and never offend our heavenly Father, who is holy and requires us to live holy (1st Peter 1:16). However, we know that when we offend Him, He is willing to forgive us when we are truly sorry and repent of our errors (1st John 1:9). We learn from our mistakes so as to not repeat them and, in so doing, continue our growth in Godly wisdom. We realize that God gives us wisdom as we meet His five requirements for wisdom;

1. **Trust God completely**
2. **Have reverence for God**
3. **Listen to our parents (obey)**
4. **Listen to God**
5. **Obey God**

****

After receiving wisdom from God, we also know that God requires us to grow in wisdom.

We grow in wisdom from the things that we experience in life, from reading and studying the Bible, and, as did the boy Jesus, by listening to and learning from the teachings of those who have Godly wisdom.

****

The need for true Christian discipleship has never been greater than it is today. More people are afraid to face the future. More people are hurting and losing all hope. More than any other time in our past, people are desperate for spiritual leadership that will meet their needs. The world is desperate for the restoration of God's power and God's unconditional and sacrificial love. This much-needed new direction in spiritual leadership from God will only occur through those who are 'just like Jesus.' People are confused about the role of the church in our society and the reality of God. They are turning in record numbers to false religions or away from all religions in the hope of finding the purpose and direction for their lives that only God can give.

Hatred among humanity is increasing not only in America but worldwide. In our current environment of racial division, social unrest, political division, and religious confusion in America and throughout the world, hope for the future of this world among children and youth is negatively affected. More than any other time in history, children and youth do not feel hopeful for their future. **As previously noted, suicides, homicides, and willful drug overdoses among children and youth are at an all-time high in America.** We see many developing troubling signs of hopelessness. However, through all of the worrisome signs, people are truly hungry for the one living and

[124]

true God that we, as disciples of Christ, love and serve. The world is desperate for the guidance and understanding of God that He will provide through those who are committed to true Biblical Christian discipleship.

As we commit our lives to God, we can become a source of hope for this world. Our journey in Christian discipleship can start at any age. We are never too old or never too young. Just like Jesus, we can begin the journey as a child. We must never limit ourselves or be discouraged by others. There is no limit to what God can do through those who love Him and are willing to totally commit their lives to Him. Paul reminded us of this fact when he wrote in Ephesians 3:20, *"Now glory be to God who by his mighty power at work within us is able to do far more than we would ever dare to ask or even dream of – infinitely beyond our highest prayers, desires, thoughts, or hopes."*

To those who are willing to trust God completely, Paul reminds us in Philippians 4:13, *"for I can do everything God asks me to with the help of Christ who gives me the strength and power."*

Christian discipleship is not easy because we live in an evil world that lives in rebellion against the living and true God that we honor. Christian discipleship will be the most difficult challenge of your life. However, the eternal rewards are more than worth the sacrifices. It can be viewed as an investment in God's kingdom and eternity.

The late evangelist Billy Graham once said, "Salvation is free, but discipleship will cost you everything you have." It will cost you friends, relationships, and the evil things and pleasures of this world. However, you will gain new friends and relationships with the correct Biblical understanding of Christian discipleship and life's meaning and purpose.

God is raising up His true army and equipping them for the end-time spiritual battles that have already started. The lives of many of America's children and youth are needlessly being lost because of a lack of Biblical spiritual knowledge and direction (Hosea 4:6), even among those who are professing Christians. Children and youth must now join God's end-time army (His remnant) and take up the blood-stained banner of Christ to provide new energy and much-needed spiritual leadership. It is now required of children and youth to help reveal the true kingdom of God on earth.

Remember, you will not be on the journey alone. The Spirit of God will be your companion and guide. Are you willing to commit to God and become just like Jesus? If so, we invite you to pray the following 'Prayer of Commitment' to our heavenly Father after answering the final questions for consideration.

As children and youth for Christ, may God forever be your guide, and you never lose hope.

Final Questions for Consideration:

1. Why must Christian disciples view themselves as soldiers and warriors?
2. What is the meaning of "persecute?"
3. Why are disciples of Christ persecuted?
4. Can you explain spiritual warfare?
5. Who is our real enemy in spiritual warfare?
6. What are the strategies of Satan in spiritual warfare? What are his goals?
7. What does it mean to remain humble?
8. How do we prepare ourselves to receive God's plan(s) for our lives?
9. List some of the requirements for Christian discipleship. Can you explain them?
10. What are some of the things that the world teaches us about life? How does the world teach us these things?
11. In contrast, what are some of the things that the Bible teaches us about life?
12. What do false prosperity ministries teach? Why are they wrong? What should be our response to them?
13. What does the Bible teach us about life's real purpose and values?
14. What is the primary duty of a Christian steward?
15. Why is Christian discipleship so important today?
16. Why should we never limit ourselves as God's servants?

* *

Yes, with God's help, I can be 'just like Jesus.'

* *

Prayer of Commitment

Heavenly Father, You are indeed a wonderful God. You have patiently waited and allowed me to come to this important point of decision in my life. You have protected me and kept me all along my life's journey. I have not been as faithful to You as You have been to me. Please forgive me.

I reach this point in my life, uncertain of what is in my future. But I am certain that my future is in Your hands. Therefore, I trust You and have hope.

As I make this commitment to You and Your kingdom, I request Your guidance from this day to the end of my service on earth. I ask that You plant a hedge of protection around my family and me to shelter us from all hurt, harm, and danger of this evil world. I ask that You forgive me of all sins in my life as I forgive all who may have sinned against me. Give me a sin-consciousness (awareness), so I will never repeat them. I truly want to serve You in all holiness. I ask that You purge my heart and give me a heart of total love for You and humanity. Give me all that is needed for this journey, for You are my provision. Mold me, make me, fill me, and use me.

Holy Father, I now commit my life entirely to You. Purge me of all worldliness and unholiness as required. I make this request and commit my life to You for Your glory. In the name of Jesus, I pray. Amen.

****

****

<u>My Life's Pledge to God</u>

I pledge allegiance to my heavenly Father
For whom I will forever stand;
one person under God,
with faith and hope for myself and all others.
I pledge, with God's help, to obey and love Him
with all my heart, soul, mind, and strength.
I pledge, with God's help, to love everyone
as Jesus loves me.
I pledge, with God's help, to obey and honor
my parents and guardians.
I know to honor them is to love them.
I will honor this pledge for the rest of my life.

Sign: _____
Date: _____

****

****

Celebrate with family and friends the beginning of your new life in Christ. Seek out others who are willing to make this commitment as your companions for this journey through life. You must never be unequally yoked with unbelievers.
(2nd Corinthians 6:14-18)

****

(We would love to hear from you regarding your new commitment. You may contact the author at penningtonwalter@bellsouth.net)

****

Though written for children and youth, this writing may also be used as a primer for "The Fanaticism of Christian Discipleship" authored by this writer.

****

Shalom

The journey continues as you grow in the image of Christ and become a reflection of His life.

Index

cross, 26, 82, 102, 112, 113, 119, 121
Daniel, 23, 33, 45
David, 78, 81
deceiver, 47, 56
deception, 34
demons, 114
destructive thoughts, 45
disciple, 1, 7, 8, 10, 11, 12, 15, 17, 26, 27, 28, 29, 30, 101, 104, 120, 121
dishonor parents 94, 95, 96
dishonor God, 18, 30
Disney, 113
disobedience, 39, 78, 79, 80
disobey, 38, 39, 93, 95
disrespectful, 103
distinct, personal will, 76, 77, 78, 79, 80, 81, 82, 83, 84, 87
distractions, 43, 50, 53, 55, 56
Divine, 14, 72, 78
donkey, 44
drug overdoses, 89, 91, 96, 124
dysfunction, 90
Egypt, 77
Elijah, 44
eternal rewards, 125
eternal salvation, 49, 115
evangelism, 71, 84
evil, 32, 34, 35, 45, 48, 53, 66, 90, 91, 97, 100, 101, 111, 112, 116, 122, 125, 126, 129
evilness, 49, 109

faith, **7**, 8, 12, 21, 22, 23, 30, 63, 65, 66, 67, 76, 83, 113, 116, 121, 131
false gods, 18, 19
false ministries, 121
Father's business, 69, 74, 75
favor, 38, 40, 72, 92, 96, 98, 106, 108
festivals, 10, 13
forgiveness, 49
forsake all, 119
foundation, 29, 66, 68
foundational, 17, 67
Gabriel, 33, 82
games, 20, 26, 50, 119
glorify, 17, 45, 49, 55, 71, 81, 84
glory, 16, 17, 55, 71, 83, 102, 103, 120, 125, 129
God's kingdom, 43, 48, 53, 59, 60, 63, 70, 74, 79, 85, 101, 102, 112, 116, 122
God's will, 28, 43, 47, 48, 75, 81, 120
God-fearing, 93
Godly wisdom, 97, 109, 120, 123, 124
gods, 18, 19, 22
Graham, Billy 125
greed, 58, 68
grow in wisdom, 35, 107, 123
hatred, 124
hear God's voice, 47, 49, 50, 53, 56
heart, 16, 17, 25, 28, 29, 30, 41, 42, 43, 47, 55, 56, 63,

[135]

Notes